Pasta! Cooking It Loving It

CARLO MIDDIONE

ILLUSTRATED BY DONALD HENDRICKS

HARPER & ROW, PUBLISHERS, New York

Cambridge, Philadelphia, San Francisco, London

Mexico City, São Paulo, Sydney

IRENA CHALMERS COOKBOOKS, INC., New York

ACKNOWLEDGMENTS

After years of believing that I had to work at things I didn't enjoy to make a living, I am forever indebted to those who have recognized my teaching and sharing of the Italian cooking that I love to do. The encouragement and support of Mary Risley, Tante Marie's Cooking School; of Ron Batori, Daniele Carlyle and Silvio D. Plaz, California Culinary Academy; of Nancy Fleming, Jack Hansen and the producers of "A.M. San Francisco"; of Harvey Steiman, Margaret Mallory, Jana Allen and others who have so kindly critiqued my work in the press; of my colleagues, my students and others too numerous to list; it is your response that makes it possible for me to engage in work as a chef. I am grateful to my family for giving me a heritage of Italian food culture and a legacy of good cooking; to Irena Chalmers for asking me to write this book about a part of it; and especially to my wife, Lisa, without whose unfailing help this book, as well as many other projects, could not have been undertaken.

FIRST HARPER & ROW EDITION

Library of Congress Cataloging in Publication Data

Middione, Carlo.
   Pasta! cooking it, loving it.

   (Great American cooking schools series)
   1. Cookery (Macaroni) I. Title. II. Series.
TX809.M17M53 1982   641.8'22   82-47861
ISBN 0-06-015068-8

82 83 84 85 86 10 9 8 7 6 5 4 3 2 1

Contents

Introduction 9

Pasta Dough 13
The Basic Fresh Pasta Dough Formula . . . 14
Making the Dough 15
Rolling the Dough 16
Colored Pastas 19

Pasta Cuts 20
*Some Considerations for Using
and Serving Pasta* 24

Boil, Boil, Toil and Trouble! 25

The Pasta Pantry 26

Recipes

Basic Sauces 30
Salsa di Pomodoro Stracotto
(SLOW TOMATO SAUCE) 30
Salsa al Pomodoro
(QUICK TOMATO SAUCE) 31
Pesto (POUNDED HERB SAUCE) 32
Salsa Bolognese, or Ragu
(BOLOGNESE MEAT SAUCE) 33
Balsamella (WHITE SAUCE) 34

Dry Pasta with Sauce (PASTASCIUTTA) 35
Spaghetti Aglio e Olio (SPAGHETTI WITH
GARLIC AND OLIVE OIL) 35

Spaghetti alla Carrettiera
(SPAGHETTI COACHMAN-STYLE) 36
Fettucine al Burro (THIN RIBBON PASTA
WITH BUTTER) 36
Fettucine al Burro e Pinoli
(THIN RIBBON PASTA WITH BUTTER
AND PINE NUTS) 36
Tagliatelle alla Bolognese (THIN RIBBON
PASTA WITH BOLOGNA-STYLE SAUCE) 37
Chiocciole al Mascarpone e Noce
(SMALL PASTA WITH CREAM CHEESE
AND WALNUTS) 37
Penne al Salmone ("PEN" MACARONI
WITH SMOKED SALMON) 38
Pasta Ericina (PASTA AS MADE
IN ERICE, SICILY) 38
Trenette con Pesto (PASTA WITH
PESTO SAUCE) 39
Pasta alla Sciacquina (PASTA
WASHERWOMAN-STYLE) 39
Maccheroni ai Quattro Formaggi
(MACARONI WITH FOUR CHEESES) 40
Pasta alla Norma (PASTA WITH
FRIED EGGPLANT) 41
Fettucine alla Romana (RIBBON PASTA
WITH CREAM, BUTTER AND CHEESE) 42
Linguine alle Vongole
(PASTA WITH CLAMS) 43

Bucatini all'Amatriciana (MACARONI WITH BACON AND TOMATO) 44

Spaghetti alla Carbonara (SPAGHETTI COAL-VENDORS' STYLE) 45

Bigoli all'Anitra (VENETIAN WHEAT PASTA WITH POACHED DUCK) 46

Paglia e Fieno (STRAW AND HAY PASTA) . . . 47

Spaghetti alla Puttanesca (HOOKERS' PASTA) 48

Spaghetti alla Viareggina (SPAGHETTI WITH CLAMS AND TOMATO) 48

Maccheroni con la Capuliata (SICILIAN MACARONI WITH GROUND MEAT) 49

Rigatoni Donnafugata 50

Pasta Arriminata (PASTA WITH BROCCOLI "STIRRED AROUND") 51

Stuffed Pasta (PASTA RIPIENI) 52

Tortellini (STUFFED RINGS OF PASTA) 52

Ravioli (STUFFED PASTA PILLOWS) 54

Agnolotti (ROUND STUFFED PASTA "LAMBS") 55

Conchiglie Ripieni (STUFFED PASTA SHELLS) 56

Cannelloni (STUFFED LARGE REEDS) 57

Pansoti con Salsa di Noce (PASTA PILLOWS OF RICOTTA WITH WALNUT SAUCE) 58

Tortelloni (Toscana) (TORTELLONI AS MADE IN TUSCANY) 59

Baked Pasta (PASTA AL FORNO) 60

Pasta al Forno (BAKED MACARONI) 60

Lasagne (BAKED FILLED PASTA SHEETS) . . . 62

Sformato di Pasta (PASTA "SOUFFLÉ") 63

Vermicelli al Forno (ULTRATHIN PASTA, BAKED) 64

Pasta in Broths and Soups (PASTA IN BRODO E MINESTRE) 65

Brown and White Stocks 65

Tagliatelle Rosa (FRESH PASTA WITH BOILED BEEF TONGUE) 66

Pastina in Brodo (LITTLE PASTA CUTS IN BROTH) 67

Tortellini in Brodo (TORTELLINI IN BROTH) 68

Minestrone alla Genovese (SOUP GENOA-STYLE) 69

Pasta e Fagioli (PASTA AND BEANS) 70

Pallotoline in Brodo (TINY MEATBALLS AND PASTINA IN BROTH) 71

Fried Pasta (PASTA FRITTI) 72

Panzarotti (FRIED RAVIOLI) 72

Frittata di Spaghetti (SPAGHETTI OMELETTE) 73

Crocchetti di Spaghetti (PASTA CROQUETTES) 74

Pasta Fritta (FRIED PASTA) 75

Sweets (DOLCE) 76

Tortelli di Ricotta (RICOTTA PILLOWS) 76

Cuscinetti di Teramo (FRIED "CUSHIONS" WITH SWEETMEAT STUFFING) 77

Cannoli Siciliana (FILLED TUBES OF PASTRY) 78

Cenci ("RAGS") 79

Wines (VINI) 80

Cheeses (FORMAGGI) 83

Introduction

Pasta is not simply flour and water or eggs. It is a way of life. Pasta knows no social, political or economic barriers or influences. It is a Godsend for the poor, and the richest of the rich have enjoyed pastas with equal gusto. Pasta may well be the most democratic food in the world, because it does the most good for the most people.

The consideration of pasta resembles a sociological study. There are Ape-Watchers, Bug-Watchers and UFO-Watchers; and there are Pasta-Watchers, of whom I am one. Thousands before me have written about pasta and there will undoubtedly be many more thousands after me. Too much, or not enough, can never be said on the subject. Perhaps the most wonderful thing about pasta is that nobody and everybody is an expert, and pasta is such an indigenous expression in Italy that there can't be any hard-and-fast rule. If you become too didactic about it, you can end up feuding with your friends and neighbors. For safety's sake, the study of pasta must be approached with a keen sense of adventure and an open mind.

In tracing the origins of pasta there are, of course, a few givens. We know that primitive man first gathered wild wheat, discovered how to hull and cook the grain and learned to mix it with water to make an edible paste. This grain paste was a staple of most prehistoric civiliza-tions, and in some form it has remained a staple ever since.

Relics from the Etruscan civilization of the 4th century B.C. show that these people had developed the tools to mix flour into dough, roll it out on a table and cut it into strips. The Latin word *nodellus*, meaning the little knot that pasta can get into if you're not careful to see that the dough isn't sticky, gave us the word "noodles." Other civilizations arrived at the same result using buckwheat, rice, soybeans, mung beans and other grains and flours.

However, over the centuries, the role of wheat pasta as a significant culinary medium has realized its highest potential in Italy. Nowhere else does pasta show up in so many guises, nowhere else has it become such a mainstay and a dietary staple as among contemporary Italians; and nowhere else has it achieved cultural expression as an indigenous form of art. Here the pristine and simple flavors of *pastasciutta* (any pasta served with sauce), butter and cheese are at one end of the scale, as they are at one end of the country, the north. The complex flavors of the delicious and earthy *pasta al forno* (baked pasta) of Sicily in the south represent the other extreme in a very broad range of applications. The pasta dish can take a primary or a secondary place in an Italian meal. Pasta can be very kind to you as a cook when you want to make a particular dish, or you can just see what you have on hand, and pasta will say, "Let's get with it!"

It is said that you can eat pasta every day of the year in Italy without repeating a single dish, and the chances are that many people do exactly that. It is estimated that 80 percent of all southern Italians eat pasta daily and some twice a day, having a *pastaciutta* (with sauce) for lunch and a *pasta in brodo* (in broth) or a *minestra* (in thick soup) for dinner or supper. Italian cooking, after all, is essentially home cooking based on available ingredients, and since pasta comes in a multitude of shapes and sizes, it is not difficult to see how this is possible.

On repeated occasions throughout the centuries, Italians have expounded different theories denouncing the abuse of pasta. Public campaigns have even been instituted against the consumption of excessive quantities of macaroni. Some "authorities" have tried to tell the Italian people that pasta was no food for fighters, for virility or for those who didn't want to get fat. However, the Italians, especially those in the south, have gone right on eating it every day. Their passion for *pastasciutta* is too deeply rooted in taste and custom. Also, a widely diffused superstition prevails that macaroni, a word today synonymous with all forms of pasta, is said to derive from the ancient Greek word *makar*, meaning "divinely holy or blessed," and is the antidote to all ills, the universal panacea.

It does seem, though, that these southern Italians know something that we don't know. Recent medical studies have reported a lower incidence of heart disease and cancer among those who eat pasta daily. A comparable study of an Italian-American "ghetto" community whose members followed a diet high in pasta and wine showed virtually no incidence of heart disease below the age of 40 and after that age an incidence of 25 percent of that found among the general United States population.

It is certainly true that one sees far fewer examples of obesity in pasta-eating Italy than in the United States, where we seem to get heavier and heavier with each national survey. With the "fitness revolution" of the 1980s, however, American media are beginning to pay increasing attention to the integral role of diet and nutrition in health and exercise programs, and to the benefits of reducing cholesterol consumption by eating more poultry and fish and less red meat and saturated fat. Nutritionists stress the importance of complex carbohydrates, especially in their unrefined forms, as focal elements in a healthy diet, because they give muscle tissue plenty of food to grow on and far less fat to worry about. An interesting scientific theory published recently reminds us that food is the usual reward for all animals, including humans, and that appetite and feeding signals are rooted in the wiring of the central nervous system. Our appetites seem to be signalling some betrayal of satisfaction from the red meat and processed foods we are feeding ourselves. The reason may be that such food fails to satisfy us until we have taken it in excessive amounts, which may well have something to do with our excess weight. The foods we currently eat are relatively new to us in evolutionary terms, because our species originally evolved on a diet of grains and fruit. Calorie for calorie, laboratory evidence shows complex carbohydrate foods are more satisfying to humans; consequently, a greater dietary emphasis upon them could well solve both our appetite problems and our excess weight.

Personally, I would almost always rather eat a normal serving of good pasta than a steak. I get more immediate satisfaction from the pasta, along with fewer calories and more peace of mind and stomach, than I possibly could from the meat. Whether made from the whole grain, or refined and enriched with fortified vitamins, the wheat flour in pasta provides a good distribution of essential amino acids to help provide protein, B vitamins (thiamine, riboflavin, and niacin) and iron. The food values are even greater in fresh egg pasta, which is considered to be one of the world's most perfect foods, because it contains virtually all of the essential nutrients. Pasta is low in fat and sodium and, if properly prepared and served, easily digested. It is an extraordinarily economical source of excellent nutrition, which can be appropriately dressed up or dressed down for almost any eating occasion.

In addition to all these paramount virtues, Italian pasta is an art object, one in which all cooks, would-be cooks and just plain eaters can find creative expression — and even humor and fun. Imaginative shapes and forms of pasta dressed in inspired sauces bring brilliant colors to the table to delight the soul and the psyche as well as the palate. When something that's good for us is so attractive and easy to take, why don't we use more of it?

Pasta is taken seriously in Italy. Per capita consumption ranges close to 70 pounds per year. In America, the last count I know of was little better than 10 pounds per person per year. However, the growing popularity of pasta in the United States will no doubt soon change this picture. Another thing that could change it even more rapidly is if Americans could learn what good pasta really is at its best, as prepared and served in Italy. That knowledge would lead to a demand for pasta of better quality in stores and restaurants, and an effort to make it properly at home.

At the risk of insulting some people, I must say that I am upset and offended by the fact that Americans often use pasta as a mere excuse for eating quarts of sauce. This only supports the myth that pasta is fattening, as most sauces surely are when taken in excess. Also, while Italians are big bread eaters, they never "double up" on wheat products at the same meal.

As a Sicilian-American, I speak from experience. I come from a long line of innkeepers. When my parents came to this country, my father – an accomplished pastry chef – operated first a café and bakery in Buffalo, New York, and later a fine dinner house and catering business in Glendale, California. My mother did the general cooking, helped by my aunts and cousins. I grew up in that kitchen and got all my practical training there.

So it saddens me that one of the first and best English language cookbooks on Italian pasta titles its chapters, "Seafood with Pasta," "Meats with Pasta," "Poultry and Game with Pasta," "Vegetables with Pasta" and even "Leftovers and Pasta." The Italian approach to pasta appears to be lost in this categorical translation, as in Italy the pasta never loses its integrity or subordinates to any sauce or accompaniment. An important standard of all good Italian cooking is to keep each ingredient unmistakably separate and to preserve each item's special characteristics rather than blending, masking, disguising or covering up textures, tastes or even blemishes. Things have to be good in themselves, without aid, to be successfully presented in an exposed and naked state. The excellence of Italian dishes depends on the excellence of the things that go into them. In the case of pasta dishes, the pasta itself is no exception to this rule. Even the popular and world-famous *Fettucine all'Alfredo* as served in the restaurants in Rome does not come to the table swimming in sauce (even though most of us *would* like to drink this ambrosia or eat it with a spoon). The pasta is beautifully coated with just the right amount of flavorful sauce. There's no question that it's pasta that you're eating, and it is just as good in and of itself as it ought to be.

Another thing that offends me is the American habit of overcooking all noodles, including pasta, in almost every serving form. If you want your pasta to be maximally digestible and to provide the greatest nutritional benefits, it must be cooked and eaten *al dente* (literally, "to the teeth," or, chewy), firm and tender. Only this way will it be chewed in the mouth, which is essential to the digestive process. Mushy and overcooked, the pasta descends to the stomach as an unmasticated solid mass, where it is quite indigestible.

Lastly, Americans must learn to eat their pasta in the approved Italian manner. If you ask for a spoon for your pasta when eating in Italy, you will be taken as an unappreciative boor and probably be effectively denied admission to the inner sanctum where Italy's most precious culinary treasures are shared. Use a fork in your right hand only. (You may use it in your left hand, as a concession, if that is natural for you.) Point it downwards and twirl it in the pasta until a reasonable amount is entwined on the fork; push a small portion away from the rest of the pasta on your plate if you need to. Now, lift the fork to your mouth and gently but firmly slurp up the ends of the pasta hanging from it. History tells us that Italians used forks in the 16th century, much earlier than the rest of Europe. It's anyone's guess how they ate their pasta before then. In Italy's Spaghetti Historical Museum, at Pontedassio near Genoa, none less than Sophia Loren's advice on etiquette is posted thus: "Spaghetti can be eaten successfully if you inhale it like a vacuum cleaner."

I remember being impressed once in a Roman restaurant by an elegant *baronessa*, in a low-cut blue dress, who complained just before dinner, *"Mi sento un' po' male"* (I feel a little poorly). She then restored her body and soul before my very eyes by eating a dish of spaghetti. When the spaghetti was set before her, she very matter-of-factly picked up her fork and plunged it into the center of the mass. She spun the fork once and then lifted it, filled with pasta, into her mouth, leaving a trail of spaghetti from her lips to the plate. From there she proceeded literally to inhale, with the most exquisite sounds of sheer appreciation I've ever heard. The strands of pasta disappeared into her mouth without a trace of splatter – if there ever was an Italian Connection, this was it. By continuous repetition of this process, the *baronessa* polished off the entire plate of pasta and, visibly improved in both appearance and mood, became even more charming than she had started out to be. After this modest beginning, she was sufficiently revivified to order and consume a *Bistecca alla Fiorentina* (a delicate Florentine-style steak) and a lovely selection of fresh fruit and some cheese, all moistened and perfumed by some delightful young Frascati white wine.

Somewhere recently my wife found a funny sticker which she posted in our kitchen at home above the Wolf range, where it's stayed ever since. It reads, "If you're not Italian, fake it!" If you want to get the most out of your pasta experience, "Fake it till you make it" may not be such bad advice for you to follow.

Pasta Dough

"A dish of pasta is only as good as the pasta itself."

LUIGI BARZINI
Author of *The Italians*

The history of Italian pasta shows its development from fresh to dried ribbons and tubes and also the industrialization of its production. Along the way, the discovery was made that hard durum winter wheat flour, rich in gluten, is stronger and superior to ordinary flour for making pasta. This dough does not fall apart in boiling water, and it is sturdy enough to hold up in a variety of fanciful shapes.

Durum wheat is a rich golden yellow with an almost nutlike flavor and a natural spicy fragrance which is sometimes likened to cinnamon. From this durum wheat is milled the *semola* or flour from which the pasta is made. *Semolina* or *semolino* is merely a coarser, more granular form of this durum flour, which consists almost entirely of the nutritious endosperm particles of the grain.

In Italy, durum flour may be purchased in the stores in a series of different grinds, from coarse to fine. Only a person with bionic arms would ever attempt to make pasta entirely by hand from semolina, the coarsest granules. In America, fine-ground durum wheat flour is not generally available in consumer markets, as it is too hard for most hand work. All the durum flour that is available is used in industrial pasta production. However, domestic and Italian imported durum Semolina (also the categorical name of the product) is increasingly available in retail stores here, and one often hears it touted these days as an essential ingredient in authentic Italian pasta. I've had so many emergency phone calls from cooking students who were unable to get their pasta dough to come together with the coarse-ground Semolina that I've come to the conclusion there may have been some slippage in the translation and usage of *semola*, or flour, and *semolina*, or grits. Another possibility is that Semolina is being offered in the United States today mainly for use with the new electric home pasta machines. At least, *they* may be strong enough to deal with it.

For centuries in Italy, pasta has been made in factories generally located in sunnier coastal areas with favorable drying conditions. Until the introduction of a continuously operated mechanical process in 1939, the work of pasta-making was organized in stages: first, mixing the flour with water or sometimes egg; next, kneading the dough; next, rolling it; and finally, cutting it. From the time of the Renaissance, the Italian pasta-making industry has been carefully controlled under increasingly rigid standards, first by guilds, then by educational institutions, now by the national government. Today, the law requires that dried commercial Italian pastas be made only with pure durum wheat flour and water, without any artificial colorings or preservatives. To develop colored pastas, only natural vegetables may be added. Dried commercial Italian egg pastas must, by law, contain at least five whole eggs for every two pounds of flour. In America, where commercial pasta is also made from durum wheat, the flour, as in our other farinaceous products, tends to be refined more in milling and thereafter enriched with fortified vitamins. American commercial egg pastas are generally made with frozen eggs or egg solids, and colored pastas are usually made with powdered dehydrated vegetables or simply vegetable dyes.

Handmade or partially handmade fresh *pasta casalinga* (homemade pasta) is still used widely in Italy. Despite the high quality of Italian commercial dried pasta today, there are many who still believe that *pasta fresca, fatt' a mano* (fresh pasta, made by hand) is the only true pasta experience. For sure, both types have their place in the pasta diet, as we shall see later on in looking at recipes. Dough formulas for fresh pasta differ from region to region in Italy. A fine grind of flour, often blending the hard wheat together with some of a softer type in order to facilitate handwork, may be mixed with egg; with egg yolk only for a very firm yellow egg pasta; with egg and a little water; or with egg and a bit of oil. The custom of adding the oil comes from Florence, and it does make the dough easier to work. However, the majority of Italians from the other regions apparently feel that oil makes the pasta too heavy; they would rather spend the extra effort necessary to obtain their first preferred result. Whole eggs are tenderizers. Some-

times the addition of a little extra egg in proportion to the flour can help out the home pasta-maker who is having difficulty working by hand. Here is the basic formula I use for good results in the United States: *One pound all-purpose flour and four large U.S. Grade A eggs yield one and a half pounds of fresh pasta.*

Alternatively, the following works very well:

The Basic Fresh Pasta Dough Formula

1. Use an all-purpose flour, *unbleached*, for a well-balanced blend of hard and soft wheat flours. It will give you a sufficiently strong pasta that you will still be able to work by hand.

2. Use three-fourths cup of flour to one large whole egg at room temperature. Because flour varies with the humidity in the climate, the altitude and other factors, and eggs also vary in size and in the way the hens that lay them have been fed, this proportion is only approximate, subject to adjustment when you have gained a feel for the optimal consistency of the dough.

3. In the kitchen we describe a batch of pasta by the number of eggs in it; that is, we make a one-egg pasta, a two-egg pasta, a three-egg pasta and so on by simply increasing the flour proportionately.

4. The one-egg pasta will yield about half a pound of fresh pasta. This will feed one person a generous main-dish serving, and possibly two persons a first-course pasta. While two ounces of commercial dried pasta are used for a first-course serving per person, remember that fresh pasta is wetter and heavier than the dried. Until you are able to gauge by eye the amount of fresh pasta to make per person, a one-egg pasta per person for a main dish, or per two persons for a first course, is a good guide.

5. In general, a three-egg pasta is about the most you will be able to make entirely by hand. Pasta-making takes a good bit of strength. For larger batches, you will probably need the aid of

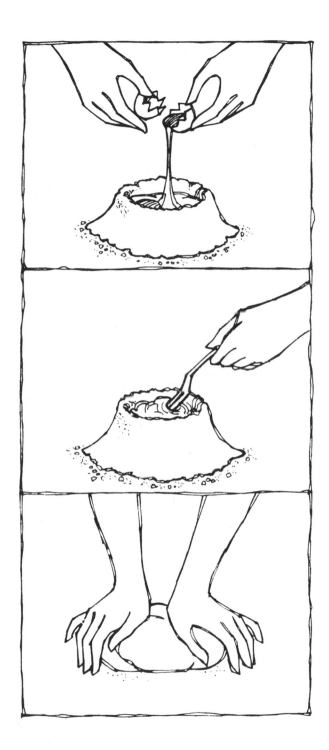

one or more machines. Even then you still may have to subdivide the batch into smaller quantities in order to work it properly.

Making the Dough

The making of pasta by hand is an art, not a science. You must make a lot of it all the time and practice constantly or you will have inconsistency in your results. It is like playing the piano or the violin or, as I have been told, sex: If you don't use it, you lose it.

By Hand

Heap the flour on a wooden or other cool surface and make a well in the center. Add the egg and immediately start to "scramble" the egg into the flour in a circular motion with a fork. Keep pushing bits of flour into the egg. When the mixture is holding together well and looks as if you can work it with your hands, do so. Knead the mass for about six or seven minutes and incorporate as much flour into it as possible. It will be very stiff and hard to work, but do it anyway. Rest frequently as needed. When properly kneaded, the dough will have a shiny look to it. Wrap it well in plastic or wax paper and let it rest for about 20 to 30 minutes on the table. *DO NOT REFRIGERATE IT!*

The kneading process is essential to a good pasta dough, as it develops the natural elasticity of the flour's gluten, which is a complex of proteins. Knead with the heel of your hand; push the ball of dough away from you; turn it a quarter turn, and repeat. Proper kneading should leave the dough smooth and silky, and at this point the gluten is so elastic that it would spring back on itself if you tried to roll it out immediately. When allowed to rest, the gluten relaxes, and the dough is then ready to be rolled out.

By Food Processor

Place the flour in the bowl. Start the blade

moving and drop in the egg. Process until the mixture looks like grains of sand. Then stop the machine; lift off the lid; take some of the mixture and squeeze it between your thumb and fingers. If it adheres to itself and forms what appears to be the beginning of a dough, empty the contents of the processor onto a board; press it together with your hands; knead and rest the dough as described. If the mixture is not moist enough to adhere to itself when you first test and squeeze it, you may add beaten egg, one teaspoon at a time, until it adheres, and then proceed as directed.

By Electric Mixer

Larger quantities of pasta dough may be made in an electric mixer. You can successfully make the dough as described by adding the eggs to the flour and using the dough hook or flat paddle attachment. This will amalgamate the flour and egg, but you will still have to knead by hand, dividing the dough into smaller portions if necessary, for at least a couple of minutes. (An exception to this, when you have become comfortable with the process, is to take the dough out in rather large lumps and *immediately* put it into manual or electric pasta rollers, which both knead somewhat as well as roll.)

By Electric Pasta Machine with Dough Hopper

Here you should follow the explicit directions of the manufacturer for both the formula of the dough and the way of making it. Your method must be compatible with the process for which the machine is designed (probably a continuous extrusion) in order to get the best results.

Rolling the Dough

By Hand

Dough to be rolled by hand should be made a bit softer by deleting one or two tablespoons of flour from the formula or by adding more egg.

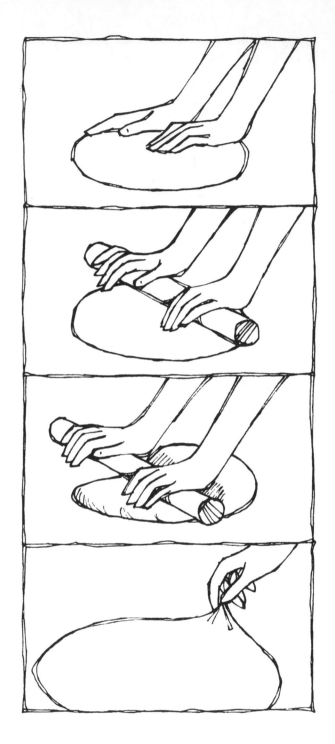

The maximum batch anybody can roll out by hand is a three-egg pasta, due to the natural limits of the length of the roller, the size of the working surface and the strength of the person. Also, hand rolling calls for a *mattarello* (roller), which is a plain long two-inch wooden cylinder that you roll with the palms of your hands. This roller has no handles or ball bearings like a regular rolling pin. The dough should be rolled on a clear piece of wood, preferably birch or pine, that is not finished in any way (no varnish or oil). The texture of the wood helps to grip the pasta and gives it an invisible patina – a lovely character, in the opinion of some people. (However, I think that's gilding the lily, and I have no objection personally to machine-rolled pasta. In fact, I make it that way all the time. The time saved enables me to do much more other cooking and more complicated cooking in addition to the pasta dish.)

Dust the surface of the board with flour and place the dough on it. Flatten the ball of dough with your hands, keeping its shape round. Put the rolling pin across the center of the dough and start to roll it away from you. Keep doing that while rotating the dough by quarters or thirds to maintain a circular shape (if it turns out to be an oval, don't worry). Remember not to compress the dough or lean on the *mattarello* while you are rolling. Just roll and stretch the dough without flattening it down. Continue with this method until the dough is as thin as you can possibly make it without tearing. It should be less than one-sixteenth of an inch. Even though it may seem very thin, remember that it will contract and thicken slightly when drying.

When the dough has reached approximately the desired thickness, you should do one little maneuver that sounds more difficult than it really is. Be sure that the dough is lightly, but evenly and sufficiently, floured. Place the *mat-tarello* at the top of the dough sheet. Pull up the top edge of the dough sheet over and around the *mattarello* and roll up about a quarter of the dough sheet (like a paper towel). Put your hands on top of the dough in the center of the *mattarello* and very quickly roll it back and forth about three to four inches. Pressing down firmly with your hands, move them apart, out across the dough, until they reach the opposite ends of the roller. Take up another quarter of the dough to the halfway mark and repeat the process. Then, unfurl the dough sheet, turn it around, and do the same steps from the other end. Repeat the full process twice. The dough is now ready for drying, prior to being cut into shapes.

Put the sheet of pasta on a large cotton or linen sheet or tablecloth, or on your cleaned and floured board. Let it air-dry for about 10 minutes on one side. Then carefully roll it up, turn it over and let it dry for a bit on the other side. The total drying time should be about 15 minutes. The dough should feel like a piece of beautiful-quality chamois leather, soft and supple, but strong and not sticky in any way. Time for drying will vary, depending upon the humidity of the air and the temperature of the room. This is only a guide. Your experience will lead you to better and better pasta every time you make it.

If this initial drying out is not done, your noodles will stick together and you will ruin all your hard work. On the other hand, if the dough dries too much, it will crumble and become unusable. A way to test the dryness of the pasta you are going to cut is to fold one edge of the sheet over on itself and squeeze it very hard. If the sheet doesn't stick and separates easily, you may have confidence that when the cuts are made, they will not stick together. When making pasta on a rainy day, be of good cheer and remember that when all else fails, you can use the hair dryer to help you out.

By Manual or Electric Pasta Rollers

Put the dough through the widest opening of the smooth rollers. Then fold it in thirds like a letter and put it through twice more. Then keep reducing the space between the rollers one notch at a time; as you put the pasta through each time, flour it as much as necessary to keep it from sticking. When it is very thin, dry as above. Use your own judgment about the thinness too. Why not take a bit and cook it in boiling water to test your result? If it is too thick, make it thinner. If it is too thin and you don't like it that way, bunch it all up and start over. Don't be afraid to experiment; this is the way you will gain precision in your results.

For my personal pasta-making at home, I use small or large Italian manual pasta-rolling machines because of my particular temperament. They do all I've ever wanted them to do, and I think my pasta is considered good. It certainly is eaten with gusto. I have several hand machines, my favorites being Excelsa and Urania in the small size, rolling about a six-inch width of pasta; and a large Imperia, which goes up to a width of nine inches. My machines have been in use for almost 20 years, but they look and work as if they were built yesterday. To get the most out of your manual pasta-rolling machine, I suggest you observe the following pointers:

1. Always secure the machine to a heavy table or counter top for maximum stability before using.

2. Separate the dough into workable portions. Never overload the machine, or it will bind or break up the dough – and start to break up its own mechanism.

3. Always start the dough in the widest open position of the rollers, turning the crank at moderate speed. Do *not* try to set world records. Be gentle but firm, and let the machine do its own work.

4. *Never* put stress on the machine. It will do all that you want it to do, but don't abuse it. If necessary, remove the piece of dough and make it a little smaller.

5. Always lower the roller setting one notch at a time to avoid straining the mechanism. The only exceptions to this are if the dough is well-kneaded beforehand, if you are in a hurry, and if your machine is well worked-in and you know its capacities. Then you may reduce the roller spaces by two at a time to facilitate speeding up the job.

6. Keep your pasta machine scrupulously clean. Use a medium-stiff dry brush to clean the rollers and all the corners and exposed parts. Brush everything thoroughly with the dry brush and use it *only* for this purpose. Then wipe the machine down with a dry cloth. Never, NEVER put any water on the machine, not even from a damp cloth, or you will destroy it in short order. Store the machine in its box in a clean location between uses.

7. If properly cleaned with dry brushes and cloths and not stressed beyond its considerable ability, your manual pasta-rolling machine will last a lifetime in perfect condition.

I have seen a home-model electric pasta-rolling machine on the market with rollers about six inches wide, made by Bialetti. Doubtless, there are others as well. If you are fortunate enough to have one, follow the manufacturer's directions scrupulously for the use and care of your machine. The procedure is essentially the same as for the manual model, but with less effort on your part, and the electric machine is even more sensitive and highly tuned than the manual. In pasta stores and restaurants, you can now see much larger electric pasta-rolling machines, which have separate hoppers for mixing and kneading the dough. However, these tend to be a bit too large for use in the average American home.

By Electric Pasta-Extruders

Home-sized continuous-process pasta-extruding machines have recently also come on the American consumer market, made by Simac, Tutto Pasta and other manufacturers. These operate on the principles of modern commercial pasta-making industrial units in Italy today, where a very strong and very firm dough is mixed and then forced into the desired shapes in one continuous process. The manufacturers of the home-sized machines of this type provide explicit directions for the dough formula, which may include hard durum wheat flour or coarse semolina, and possibly some water in addition to the eggs in the egg pasta formula. If the directions compatible with the particular machine are carefully followed, you will be able to make excellent pasta of the extrusion type with very little practice. Such machines could be especially desirable for pasta-lovers living in areas where the shapes they want are not available, or where good, dried pastas are hard to find. With a minimum amount of experience or work, you should be able to get reliably good results.

Colored Pastas

At the risk of being branded as a heretic, I must tell you that I consider colored pastas, at most, a gimmick. I, for one, am so busy trying to make, to teach and to eat a truly fine natural egg pasta as a classic *casalinga* (homemade) type that I haven't time to worry about gilding the lily. The only time I ever encountered colored pasta in Italy in a public eating place was in Umbria. The pasta was rose-colored, probably from beets, and the color made little difference to my enjoyment of the pasta dish or to my palate's satisfaction. In my opinion it is aesthetically and gastronomically unnecessary to worry about colors in your home-made pasta, with the possible exception of green spinach noodles, which are a nice occasional variation. In a blindfold test, I would not be able to tell the difference in taste between a colored and a plain pasta, except that colored pasta is too often soft and inferior in texture.

If you want to try making some colored pasta, you will find it easier to mix the dough with a food processor than by hand. Take about a half cup of cooked spinach, tomato or whatever vegetable color you want and squeeze it as dry as you can in paper towels. (This is easier if you have steamed the vegetable in as little water as possible.) You can also dry it by tossing it in a dry frying pan, or use the hair dryer; better yet, cook it the day before and let it air-dry overnight. Puree the vegetable in the food processor; add the flour and mix well before adding the egg, as a guide to the amount of egg the mixture will take. You may have to reduce the amount of egg lest the dough become too soft. Dried vegetable powders pulverized to the fineness of face powder are used in making commercial colored pastas. If they ever become available on the consumer market, it will be possible to make colored pasta at home with more reliable results. Once the dough is made, colored pasta-making proceeds exactly as the plain.

Incidentally, my remarks about colored pasta do not apply to the natural whole wheat pasta used a lot in and around Venice. To make this, try replacing up to 70 percent of the unbleached white flour in your formula with whole wheat flour, and proceed as usual. You will have to develop the right amounts on an ad hoc basis, incorporating as much whole wheat as the pasta will take.

Pasta Cuts

Since its basic primitive beginnings, Italian pasta has acquired an almost bewildering variety of shapes and forms which are used in countless different ways. No other food in history comes to mind which has ever been applied in a fraction of so many versions. How and why this came to pass is difficult to know for sure.

Perhaps it is due in part to the fundamental diversity of the Italian people, who were only unified by Garibaldi into one nation in the 1860s. The differences among the Italians even today are seen by sociologists as far greater in extent and more fundamental in kind than among the inhabitants of any other country of comparable size. All Italians have in common, however, a profound respect for good, basic food ingredients, perhaps because in their over-populated homeland these have always been in short supply.

Another reason for the many riotous shapes of pasta may be that the Italians are always ready to rejoice in *abbondanza* (plenty) when it comes to food, because it represents to them the joy of living and the goodness of life. Even medical studies of the remarkable health of Italian pasta-eaters comment on their deep enjoyment of the food they eat as a significant element of their general well-being.

To get to know the hundreds of cuts and shapes of Italian pasta is no small undertaking.

The challenge is compounded by the fact that the same shapes may be called by different names in different parts of Italy. If you're eating tagliatelle in Bologna, your counterpart in Rome would be eating fettucine – exactly the same ribbon cut. There are legends galore about how the pasta shapes developed; of coure, everyone knows that the stuffed tortellini was originally modeled after Venus's navel.

Suffice it to say that all people of all ages like, at times, to play. A little knowledge can be a dangerous thing, but at the risk of oversimplifying an approach to describing Italy's hundreds of pasta cuts, let's start out with the simplest and best-known shapes we can make ourselves or obtain readily in America.

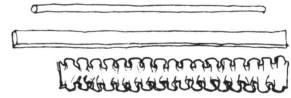

Flat Ribbon Pastas

From the narrowest strip you can cut up to a width of about one and one-half inches, you can call your flat ribbon pastas:

> *Lingue di passero* (sparrow's tongues)
> *Bavettine* (collar or tie)

Linguine (tongues)
Bavette (larger collar, at least one-eighth inch wide)
Tagliarini (shreds) or *Fettucine* (ribbons)
Trenette (trains) or *Lasagnette* or *Fettucine* (a larger, alternative ribbon)
Lasagne (possibly means clumsy, from "dolt"; up to one and one-quarter inch to one and one-half inch wide) Note that in the past, *lasagne* were sometimes square or oblong pieces of pasta dough, often with rippled edges, which were layered at random with the filling of the baked *lasagne* dish.

You will probably find a couple or three of these widths among the dies supplied with your manual or electric pasta-rolling machine. To make these ribbon pastas, simply take your pasta sheets, prepared and dried as directed, and run them through the rollers with the desired die attachment. To make the very narrow and very wide widths for which no dies are available, roll up your pasta sheet loosely in the shape of a roll of paper towels, and cut across it with a knife by hand to the width desired. You can, of course, hand cut all of the widths if you don't have the rollers and dies.

One word of caution: *Never* make your fresh ribbon pastas more than twelve inches long, as they will bind up during cutting. Don't worry about waste in trimming up your pasta sheets, as there is a use for the scraps known as *malfatti* (poorly made), which can be dried and set aside to be used in broths and soups. Also, if you wish, you can use a fluted wheel dough-cutter to crimp the edges of your larger ribbons and lasagne for a more finished look.

Once cut, your ribbon pastas may be cooked at once and eaten fresh; dried (hung on the back of a chair, a towel rack or any similar arrangement), floured as necessary and cooked later; or dried, floured (some prefer to use rice flour, as it's drier than wheat flour) and stored. Fresh egg pasta may be kept in the refrigerator for two days. If *completely* dried and placed in a bag or a box, it can be stored for about as long as commercial pasta.

Pasta Tubes and Rods, Long and Short

In the old days, tube pastas were made in Italy by wrapping a long, narrow width of pasta lengthwise around a knitting needle, pressing the flap to seal it closed and then withdrawing the needle. I've not personally seen anyone do this by hand in Italy or America. However, on my last trip to Italy I did find a charming old lady making *garganelli* (gulps or bites), sometimes called *pasta alla pettine* (pasta made on a comb), by hand in a small pasta shop in Imola, near Bologna. This is a short pasta rolled diagonally around a small, round pointed wooden stick against a *pettine* (a cane comb), which gives it a slightly *rigati* (grooved) texture. It is actually a small *mostaccioli* (mustache), a name better known in America. The old lady made me a gift of one of her own stick-and-comb sets, but I, like most others, lack the time for such detailed hand production. She, of course, made the *garganelli* from small strips of dough with dazzling speed.

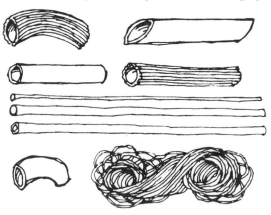

Rods and tubes are made in commercial dried pastas in Italy today by the industrial continuous-extrusion process. Some of the same shapes can be found in commercial dried American pastas. Some of them can be made fresh at home with the electric pasta-extrusion machines (check their available dies). Rods and tubes include the following long shapes from small to large:

Capellini (hairs; cylindrical pasta, very tiny)
Vermicelli (worms, a little larger)
Spaghettini (small strings, still cylindrical)
Spaghetti (normal strings, a little larger)
Bucatini (pierced) or *Fischetti* (whistles, smallest of the tubes)
Perciatelli (tubes)
Macaroni (tubes, a bit larger)
Ziti (large tubes)
Ziti Rigati (large tubes, grooved)

Then there are the short cylinders and tubes with plain or grooved texture:

Bombolotti (short, smooth cylinders)
Penne (quills, diagonal tubes)
Mostaccioli (mustaches, diagonal tubes)
Rigatoni (grooved tubes)

There are also the curved short "elbows," which may be made from any of these shapes.

Fancy-Shaped Pastas

With the exception of the *farfalle* (butterflies) and *fiochetti* (small bows, bow ties), which are pinched from flat pieces and can be made by hand if you have the time, these fancy concave shapes are best made today by machines which force the extruded dough into special dies:

Lumache (snail shells)
Capelli di Preti (small priests' hats)
Conchiglie (seashells, several sizes from small to jumbo)

Creste di Galli (cocks' combs)
Fusilli (twists)
Rotelle (wheels)

To make the butterflies and bows by hand, cut rectangular pieces from your pasta sheet approximately two inches by one inch, using a fluted wheel if you want a fancy edge, and simply pinch them together in the middle. You can also round the corners of the rectangles if you wish. Dry 30 to 40 minutes before cooking.

Small Pastas for Broths and Soups

It would not make sense to attempt the tiniest pastas by hand, and a large number of them tend to be generally available in either Italian imported or American commercial dried pasta. They can add a great deal to broths and soups. Remember one thing, however; these pastas should always be cooked separately in plain water to the al dente stage and *then* added to the broth or soup just before serving. If you try to cook them in the soup, they may absorb too much of your soup's liquid and/or become quite overcooked and mushy. Here is a list of some of the popular and best known tiny pastas.

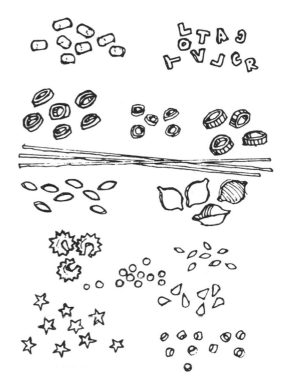

Clearly, pastas are named for their shapes, and this category opens a world of imaginative educational opportunities for children. One soup pasta that you can make by hand is *pasta gratugiata* (grated pasta), because of its less well-defined shape. Prepare fresh egg pasta dough; let it rest 10 minutes; then grate it on a flat grater. Let the gratings rest 40 minutes; then cook them and add to your soups. This is another excellent way to use up pasta trimmings, also.

Stuffed Pastas

Some of the *pasta ripieni* (stuffed pastas) that make a major contribution to the Italian pasta repertory:

> *Cappelletti* (little hats as worn by bishops and cardinals)
> *Agnolotti* (round ravioli)
> *Cannelloni* (large reeds)
> *Manicotti* (small muffs)
> *Ravioli* (shaped as small, square pillows)
> *Tortellini* (small filled rings)

With fillings of cheese, spinach, meat or chicken, and with sauces, these pastas make excellent

Acini di Pepe (peppercorns)
Alfabeto (letters of the alphabet)
Anelli (rings)
Anellini (little rings)
Anellini Rigati (grooved rings)
Capelli d'Angelo (angels' hairs)
Cappelli de Pagliaccio (clowns' hats)
Chicchi di Riso (grains of rice)
Conchigliette or *Maruzzine* (tiny shells)
Coralli (coral)
Funghini (little mushrooms)
Orzo (barley)
Pastina (tiny dough)
Perline Microscopici (tiny pearls)
Pulcini (little chickens)
Semi di Mele (apple seeds)
Semi di Melone (melon seeds)
Stellini (little stars)
Tubettini (tiny tubes)

and appropriate main-dish meals. They can and should be made fresh from sheets of egg pasta dough *before* it has been dried, and the results are definitely worth the extra effort. All of them start with circles or squares of pasta which are rolled or pressed around the fillings and fashioned into their special shapes (see Stuffed Pastas, page 52).

There are now pasta stores and Italian delicatessens in many American communities where these stuffed pastas can be bought freshly made. Some of them are also available in the supermarkets as frozen prepared dishes. There are a couple of other options available to you to assemble at home. Manicotti shells can be bought in commercial dried pasta, sometimes specially treated so that they need not be boiled before stuffing and baking. I've tried these and they are not bad, especially for entertaining in larger numbers when you are short of time to make your own by hand. Also the jumbo shells (conchiglie) and the large tubes (ziti), if locally available to you in commercial dried pasta, can be boiled and then filled with delicious fresh homemade stuffing, sauced, and baked with highly successful results (see recipe on page 56).

Gnocchi

Gnocchi, or dumplings, were possibly the first primitive pasta shapes ever made. However, today gnocchis are made of so many things other than pasta dough (potatoes, ricotta cheese, polenta, semolina, and so on) that I am not including them in this pasta collection.

SOME CONSIDERATIONS FOR USING AND SERVING PASTA

- Fresh pasta, which (especially when rolled) is distinctively firm and springy yet deliciously tender, will absorb sauces more readily than commercial dried pasta.
- The delicacy of fresh pasta deserves the lightest, least assertive saucing.
- Tubular and concave pasta shapes are actually designed to trap sauces. Use them when you want to eat a lot of sauce in each bite.
- A delicate sauce is best served with a delicate pasta.
- A rich sauce should be served with a flat pasta, or a shape which will not trap or accumulate too much of the sauce in each bite.
- The taste of pasta will vary with the thickness and texture of its particular cut.
- While one school of thought holds that you should drink water with pasta and no wine until afterwards, the majority of Italians enjoy wine together with pasta.
- The wines to accompany pasta dishes are chosen to go well with the particular sauce used. In Italy a wine of the same region as the pasta dish is generally used.

Italians have brought the making and eating of pasta to a fine art. The more deeply you become involved in the experience yourself, the better you will be able to orchestrate the broad range of opportunities pasta offers to satisfy your own taste and enjoyment of eating.

Boil, Boil, Toil and Trouble!

The first two words are correct. We'll dispense with the others as inaccurate. Here are some of the golden rules that will get you through the cooking of pasta with no toil or trouble.

1. Use lots of water, so that the pasta can float freely while cooking. You should allow at least four to five quarts of water per pound of pasta. Too little water prevents the pasta from cooking evenly, and the pieces may stick together as a result.

2. Bring the water to a galloping boil.

3. When the water is boiling briskly, add some salt, preferably noniodized. (If the salt is added before the water boils, it may leave a residual taste of phenol on delicate pastas.)

4. Put in the pasta. Long pastas should be in manageable lengths. The commercial dried pastas, especially, will grow larger during cooking. To get very long pastas into the pot, grasp a bundle of them at one end; submerge the other end of the bundle in the boiling water; as the submerged end of the pasta bundle softens, gradually release your hold and the rest of the bundle of long pastas will slide into the pot of boiling water without breaking.

5. Watch the pasta. Fresh homemade egg pasta will cook in seconds or minutes. Commercial dried pastas can take nearly 20 minutes, depending on size. You can be guided to some extent by the directions on the package, but it is still essential to watch the pasta very closely as it cooks and to test it frequently for doneness.

6. Pasta is done when it tests al dente (to the tooth), is tender but firm, still biteable and not mushy, but with no taste of flour.

7. Remove the pasta from the boiling water immediately. It can be lifted out of the water with a pasta rake or a slotted spoon, or it can be drained in a colander.

8. Pasta to be served with a sauce should be eaten immediately. The sauce should be ready and waiting. The bowls or plates should be hot. Toss the pasta in some of the sauce (use a separate hot serving bowl, or the empty pot in which it was cooked), serve it and pass additional sauce or cheese.

9. Boiled pasta to be baked should be *undercooked* in the boiling, as it will be cooked more later in the baking sauce. Also, it can be cooled and the boiling arrested by plunging the pasta into cold water. This is the one and only type of cooking in which you would do this to the pasta.

The Pasta Pantry

Only recently I learned something I never knew before, although I have been cooking all my life. The word *recipe* is not an English or French word, as I had always believed, but actually the Latin word for "procure" in its imperative form. This suggests the functions of marketing and the *mis en place* in French or *a posto* in Italian, or the assembly of ingredients so critical to the working cook.

I want to suggest a few basic items for you to stock up on. You may want to keep the non-perishables on hand regularly. You would probably also be wise to identify sources for the perishables where you will be able to find them when you need them instead of finding yourself stuck at the last minute. If there are no stores where you live that carry the special Italian items, look at a copy of one of the consumer gourmet magazines, and you will probably find an advertised source from which you can order by mail. Many of the imported specialties have become quite expensive. However, most of them are well worth whatever you can afford to pay, as remarkably small quantities will go a long way toward giving the true taste of Italy to your pasta dishes. Of course, I think you should have imported *parmigiano*. But I would rather have you make the dishes with the materials you have at hand and appreciate the concept of the recipe, even though you might miss the high points in flavor that are to be derived from using the original ingredients. (Not everyone can go to see the Mona Lisa, but a reasonable facsimile can still activate some of the emotional machinery needed to have a satisfying experience.)

Everyday Items

Flour, all-purpose unbleached
Milk
Eggs
Butter
Salt
Whole black pepper for fresh grinding
Heavy cream
Garlic
Onions
Scallions
Breadcrumbs (plain)

Tinned Goods

Tomatoes, canned. The 28-ounce (1-pound, 12-ounce) size is most useful. Test to make sure you find a reliable brand with a thick pureed pack, *not* a watery pack.
Tomato paste. Tubes are handy and keep well in the refrigerator after opening.
Tomato puree
Tuna, packed in oil. The imported Italian variety, if you can find it, is definitely worth the cost.

Anchovy fillets, packed in salt if available, or packed in oil.

Capers, the large Spanish type if possible, bulk-packed in salt, if you can find them.

Chopped clams – and make sure they are not sandy.

Olive oil, domestic, for most cooking

Olive oil, imported Italian or French extra-virgin, at least a small amount for accent.

Herbs, Spices and Nuts

In general in this category, fresh herbs are more pungent than dried; whole spices freshly ground are much more flavorful than those already ground up; nuts should be as fresh as possible and kept in the freezer for best storage.

Basil, as in sweet basil
Bay leaf
Fennel seed
Oregano
Sage
Nutmeg
Red chili peppers, dried
White pepper
Pine nuts (shelled)
Walnut meats

Specialties and Fresh Items

Pancetta. Italian-style salt-cured (unsmoked) bacon. If you can't find it, regular bacon may be used after first poaching it in water for a few minutes to reduce the smoky flavor; or

lean salt pork soaked in cold water for an hour to remove some of the salt.

Prosciutto, the Italian-style ham, also cured with salt and unsmoked. Have it thinly sliced at the store. It is not permitted to be imported from Italy, but Hormel makes an excellent prosciutto here.

Mortadella, an Italian-style boiled sausage, thinly sliced

Olives, Sicilian black or Calamata. Unfortunately American commercially packed olives do not approach their taste and will not give you the result you want in the recipes calling for olives.

Dried *porcini* mushrooms, imported from Italy and well worth the price. In case you enjoy wild mushroom hunting, these are the *boletus edulis* species which can be found in a lot of areas in the United States.

Sweet butter (quite perishable unless kept in the freezer)

Fresh Italian parsley

Spinach. Fresh is best; frozen will do in some cases

Red and green peppers, in season

Cream cheese

Cheeses

Parmesan, best imported, aged two years. Buy this in the piece. It will keep well in the refrigerator for several months. Grate it *only* when you are ready to use it.

Parmesan, domestic, reasonably priced, good for pasta fillings and baked dishes; but do try to get it in the piece, too, and grate it freshly each time you use it.

Ricotta. A good local source for this lovely cheese is a must. Ricotta looks a little like cottage cheese, but it's lighter, fluffier and sweeter.

Romano, domestic, made from cow's milk, or Pecorino, imported from Italy, made from sheep's milk. They are hard, for grating, and store well. Quite salty, but good in certain dishes.

Mozzarella, the stringy cheese, still made from the milk of the water buffalo in Italy. Domestic mozzarellas can be fine, as made here from cow's milk. A soft jack will also serve. For more on Italian cheeses, see page 83.

Wines

Pasta dishes, being fairly light for the most part, call for uncomplicated dry, young white and red wines. Of course, there are exceptions to this as there are to all rules, and some pastas certainly can stand up to heavier and more full-bodied wines. Most of the large production of Italian wine fits the major criterion for use with pasta dishes, in that this wine is generally made to be drunk while young, with little or no aging. More and more of the regional wines of Italy are now being imported. They tend to be well priced and quite suitable for use with pasta here, just as they are used in Italy. Among the California wines, I would personally choose some of the *vini di casa* (everyday wines of the house) or the jug wines now becoming so popular and so reasonable as well. Most of the finer and more expensive California premium wines are literally too big, too self-important and too precious to be used with most pasta dishes. I prefer to reserve them to enjoy with other types of food, or just on their own. I know that there are now more and more good wines being grown in other parts of the United States as well, but so far, I am not very familiar with them.

In the pasta recipes I will give you some wines by generic names or types. You should find that sufficient to help you buy the ones I suggest as the most suitable. Your own taste will surely differ from mine. Buy accordingly.

For more on Italian wines, see page 80.

Recipes

Basic Sauces

Salsa di Pomodoro Stracotto *(SLOW TOMATO SAUCE)* *Makes 2½ quarts*

This is the classic approach to the richer, heavier and traditionally darker-colored tomato sauce, which is cooked slowly for a long time. In Italy, fresh sun-ripened tomatoes, usually the smaller pear-shaped type, are preserved for use between seasons by sun-drying, which is preferred to canning. The fresh tomatoes are split, lightly salted, strung into ropes and hung outdoors until dried naturally by sun and air. Reconstituted in water, these dried tomatoes make the best traditional sauce of all.

If good fresh tomatoes are available to you, use the same weight as that given for the canned tomatoes in the recipe and prepare as directed in the Quick Tomato Sauce. With this slow-cooked sauce, however, I recommend you do take the trouble to remove the seeds.

Many people complain about tomatoes being too "acid," not sweet enough, even the canned ones, that are supposed to be picked ripe. I am not put off by it if, in fact, the tomatoes do taste a bit acid. There are many times in cooking when the acid effect of the tomato on other ingredients will give you exactly the result you want. I rather like this because it is so subtle.

Remember that a tomato, while classified as a fruit, is still not a peach. If you find the flavor of your tomatoes too sharp, do not add sugar, as you are often counselled to do. Instead, add two or three times the amount of onion called for in the recipe – but cook it first, if not added at the beginning. You will be surprised at how sweet your tomato sauce will become from the natural sugar in the onions, and no one will be able to guess that you have a lot of onions in it. Somehow, added sugar in tomatoes can always be identified and is often unpleasant to the taste. The onions, on the other hand, blend and integrate so well in this slow cooking that they cannot be tasted as such. The whole sauce tastes just wonderful.

4 tablespoons olive oil
1 large yellow onion, finely chopped
3 garlic cloves, finely chopped
2 1-pound, 12-ounce cans tomatoes, coarsely chopped
1 cup water
1 cup red wine
4 tablespoons tomato paste
Sprig of fresh oregano or 1 teaspoon dried
Salt and pepper to taste

Heat the oil in a wide heavy pan and fry the onion until soft and transparent. Add the garlic and fry until golden. Add all other ingredients. Cook uncovered on a very slow fire at a simmer for 3 hours. Stir occasionally. Use on baked pasta or on big stubby boiled pasta.

Salsa al Pomodoro *(QUICK TOMATO SAUCE)*

Makes 2 generous quarts

This is a fresh-tasting, almost tart sauce that is excellent for pasta. It is also known as Salsa alla Marinara *(Sailor Sauce). The same weight of fresh tomatoes may be used, and if they are sun-ripened and naturally sweet as they should be, the taste of the sauce will benefit greatly. Before starting the sauce, prepare the tomatoes by chopping them up and putting them through the food mill to remove skin and seeds. If you don't mind the seeds, you can skin the tomatoes before chopping and then use them directly in the recipe.*

However, unless the fresh tomatoes are truly fine, you are better off using good canned ones. Immature fresh tomatoes without well-developed fruit sugars will do nothing to improve this sauce and will more likely detract from its flavor.

1 large yellow onion, finely chopped
¼ cup good olive oil
2 medium-size garlic cloves, finely chopped
2 1-pound, 12-ounce cans tomatoes, finely chopped
Sprig of fresh oregano or 1½ teaspoons dried
4 leaves fresh basil or 1½ teaspoons dried
Salt and pepper to taste
Optional: Pinch crushed red pepper

Put the chopped onion in a wide heavy pan and add the olive oil. Cook until transparent; then add the garlic. Cook about 3 minutes more; add all other ingredients and cook on a brisk flame about 15 minutes, stirring occasionally. (The optional pinch of crushed red pepper may be added whenever a more profound taste is desired.) The fast cooking will help to reduce the sauce and make it thick, but be careful that it does not burn on the bottom.

NOTE: The same base can be used in making fish stew, in which case add ⅓ cup or more of white or red wine before cooking and the fish and shellfish just minutes before serving.

Pesto *(POUNDED HERB SAUCE)*

Serves 4

The traditional Pesto *from Genoa is delicious alone as a topping for pasta. It can also be used as a decorative dressing for sliced hard-boiled eggs served as an appetizer; as a sauce for grilled meats or fish; as a sauce for sun-ripe sliced fresh tomatoes; in salads, in omelettes, and in whichever other ways an adventurous taste exploration would elect. Pesto is also sometimes made with fresh parsley (Italian parsley is the best) if basil is not available.*

Fresh pesto should be used immediately. However, I have suggested a way of preserving this delicious sauce when you are taking advantage of the fresh basil season to make it in quantity to store for future use.

1 cup fresh basil leaves, tightly packed
1 garlic clove, thumb-sized
1 heaping tablespoon Parmesan cheese, best quality, freshly grated
1 tablespoon freshly grated Romano cheese
1 teaspoon fresh shelled pine nuts (or optional walnuts)
⅔ cup olive oil (adjust less or more, depending on desired thickness of pesto)
Salt and pepper to taste

Run the ingredients on the cutting blade of the food processor, adding them in the order given, taking pains to extract maximum juice and flavor from each ingredient. Withhold the olive oil until the other ingredients are well blended into a paste. Then add the oil gradually, mixing constantly, until the sauce has reached the consistency desired. Season to taste with salt and pepper.

The sauce was originally made by hand in a mortar and pestle, but a food processor does an adequate job; a blender is less satisfactory because you may have to add the oil too soon.

Boil and sterilize a Mason jar. Fill it with pesto, leaving a good inch empty below the top of the jar. Cover the surface of the sauce with a good half-inch layer of olive oil, to keep the air from the surface. Place in the refrigerator. *Do not freeze!* Pesto stored this way can be kept for months and may even improve with age. To use, scoop out the desired amount, bring up to room temperature, stir well and add olive oil as needed.

Be sure to add fresh olive oil to the surface of the pesto still in the jar to protect it from the air and return the remaining supply promptly to the refrigerator.

Salsa Bolognese, or Ragu

(BOLOGNESE MEAT SAUCE)   *Makes about 2½ cups*

In America this is the most popular and best known of the famous Italian Ragu *(meaning literally stew) meat sauces. While purists know that the* Ragu *starts with a solid piece of meat, hand-cut with care by a knife or even snipped with a kitchen scissors into tiny morsels, ground meat is used here for convenience. After long cooking in the sauce, one can hardly tell the difference in how the meat was cut up. Try it both ways, with ground or hand-cut meat, and adopt the result you like best.*

2 ounces prosciutto fat or pancetta, finely chopped
1 medium-size carrot, finely chopped
1 tender yellow branch of celery, including leaves, finely chopped
¾ pound ground round
½ whole clove
1 cup red wine
½ cup cream
1 teaspoon salt
⅛ teaspoon pepper
1 cup finely chopped fresh tomatoes, or canned, including juice

Put the prosciutto fat or pancetta in a heavy pan and cook it until it melts. Add onion, carrot and celery. When the mixture gets a light golden color, add the meat, breaking it up with a fork, and cook, stirring frequently, until it just loses its pink color. Add the ½ clove and the red wine. Cook on a brisk flame until the wine evaporates, or about 10 to 15 minutes. Add the cream and lower the flame; cook gently until the cream practically disappears, then add the salt and pepper to taste. Add tomatoes and cook gently for about 2 hours, stirring occasionally.

The result should be a thick and lovely mass resembling a puree. This can be used as a sauce on tagliatelle or other pasta. It will keep in the refrigerator for 4 to 5 days, and it also freezes and holds well.

Balsamella *(WHITE SAUCE)*

Makes 1 pint

This is a simple and reliable basic white sauce, widely useful in general cooking as well as in pasta. Known as Béchamel *in French cooking, the sauce actually originated as* Balsamella *in Italy long before the 16th century, when Catherine de Medici brought it to France.*

Learning to make a really good Balsamella sauce comprehends principles of cooking with many other valuable applications. Infusing milk with herbs and spices before using in almost any recipe will add rich and subtle flavor to your dish. Learning to "tamp" finished food from the air with parchment paper is a wonderful way to hold many foods back. A good Balsamella can turn simple ingredients into an elegant feast. Buon appettito!

2 cups milk
3 tablespoons butter
3 tablespoons flour
Salt and white pepper to taste
Optional: grating of nutmeg; slice of onion; clove of garlic; bay leaf.

Heat the milk in a saucepan and infuse it with any or all of the optional flavorings (or none, if you want a very bland-tasting sauce) by simply dropping in the herbs and spices. Do not let the milk boil. Keep it hot.

In another saucepan melt the butter over medium heat; when it is melted and bubbling, add the flour all at once, stirring constantly with a whisk. Let the mixture cook for a couple of minutes, but watch that it doesn't burn or scorch. Take it off the flame for a moment and then add the hot milk, straining it all at once through a small sieve, while stirring the whole time. Put the sauce back on the heat. Cook and stir constantly until it begins to boil. Then lower the heat, cook and stir until it is thick and glossy. Use it immediately.

NOTE: If you do not wish to use this sauce right away, butter a piece of parchment or wax paper and push it right down onto the surface of the sauce, pressing the paper tightly against the sides of the pan to keep all the air off the surface. You can store it like this for several days in the refrigerator, and the sauce will not "skin over" because it has been protected from the air. When you are ready to use it, simply remove the paper, place the sauce on the heat and stir it until it is hot and glossy.

You can also make the sauce thinner or thicker simply by adding more or less of the liquid or solid ingredients. If the sauce is too thick, add a little hot milk and mix well, returning it to the heat for a bit, if necessary. If the sauce is too thin, cook it longer over slow heat, but be careful not to let it scorch.

Dry Pasta with Sauce
(Pastasciutta)

Spaghetti Aglio e Olio
(SPAGHETTI WITH GARLIC AND OLIVE OIL)   *Serves 4 to 6*

This is a famous, simple pasta which many Italians call their favorite. Some say they eat it when they feel sad because it makes them feel happy again. Well, garlic is supposed to have curative powers.
   Wine suggested: A Barbera or a Gattinara.

½ cup olive oil
4 large garlic cloves, finely chopped
1 pound spaghetti, fresh or dried
½ cup finely chopped parsley
Freshly ground or cracked
   black pepper
Optional: Pinch of crushed red
   pepper flakes

Place the oil and garlic in a pan and cook until light golden in color. Cook spaghetti al dente (see page 24). When pasta is done, drain it well and put it into a warm serving bowl. Add the parsley to the oil and garlic. Pour the mixture on the pasta and mix well. Sprinkle on the freshly ground or cracked black pepper and serve very hot. As an option you can throw on a good pinch of red pepper flakes at the time of mixing. No cheese on this, please!

Spaghetti alla Carrettiera (SPAGHETTI COACHMAN-STYLE) *Serves 3 or 4*

This is another version of pasta with garlic, this time together with the salty cheese, Pecorino, used as a daily staple by people who need all the energy they can possibly develop.
   Wine suggested: A Barbera or a Gattinara.

3 large garlic cloves,
   finely chopped
¼ cup olive oil
1 generous cup chopped parsley
1 good pinch red pepper flakes
Salt and pepper to taste
12 ounces spaghetti, fresh or dried
½ cup freshly grated Pecorino
   (Romano) cheese

Gently brown the garlic in the oil, being careful not to burn it. Add the parsley, red pepper and salt and pepper to taste.
   Boil the pasta al dente (see page 24). When the pasta is done, drain it and add it to the garlic and oil mixture. Toss well. Add cheese, toss again and serve very hot.

Fettucine al Burro *(THIN RIBBON PASTA WITH BUTTER)* *Serves 4 to 6*

This is the very simple way in which many Northern Italians prefer to enjoy their pasta.
   Wine suggested: A Sauvignon Blanc or a Soave.

6 ounces unsalted butter
1 pound fresh fettucine
½ cup freshly grated
   Parmesan cheese
Freshly ground black pepper

Place butter in a warm serving dish to become very soft. Cook pasta al dente (see page 24). Drain and immediately transfer to the dish with butter, and toss gently. Add cheese and toss gently again. Grind on the pepper. Serve at once, hot! Pass more cheese at the table.

FETTUCINE AL BURRO E PINOLI
(THIN RIBBON PASTA WITH BUTTER AND PINE NUTS) *Serves 4 to 6*

1 recipe Fettucine al Burro
5 tablespoons pine nuts

Gently brown the pine nuts in a heavy skillet using no butter or oil, stirring them continuously. Watch out, they burn *very* fast! When golden in color, remove them immediately from the flame. Put them aside in a small dish and proceed with the recipe above, except that you will add the pine nuts at the same time as the cheese. A delicious dish!

Tagliatelle alla Bolognese
(THIN RIBBON PASTA WITH BOLOGNA-STYLE SAUCE)

Serves 4

This classic pasta from Bologna, considered by many to be the "food capital" of northern Italy, is best eaten in its home town, but you can achieve delicious results here if you don't oversauce it.
Wine suggested: A California Grignolino or a Lambrusco.

2½ cups Salsa Bolognese (see page 33)
12 ounces fresh tagliatelle, or more
½ cup or more freshly grated Parmesan cheese

Heat the sauce and keep it hot. Cook the tagliatelle al dente (see page 24), and drain it well. Put on a little of the sauce and mix thoroughly. Serve on a warm plate with a ladleful of sauce on top. Pass the cheese at the table.

Chiocciole al Mascarpone a Noce
(SMALL PASTA WITH CREAM CHEESE AND WALNUTS)

Serves 6

This is an elegant first-course pasta that should be eaten in small amounts. It is one of the many wonderful Italian pasta dishes which are still relatively unfamiliar in America.
Wine suggested: A Gamay Beaujolais or a Freisa.

1½ tablespoons butter
6-8 ounces Mascarpone cheese
12 ounces dried "shell" pasta, 1-inch size
3 tablespoons freshly grated Parmesan cheese
2-3 ounces walnut meats, coarsely chopped

Melt the butter over low heat in a fireproof serving dish. Add the cheese and melt it slowly. Do not let it boil.

Cook the pasta al dente (see page 24). Drain it when done, leaving a few spoonfuls of water in it. Add it to the cheese and butter mixture and stir it all around. Add the grated Parmesan cheese and the walnuts and mix again. Serve hot, garnished with a few larger pieces of walnut if you like, and pass some more freshly grated Parmesan at the table.

NOTE: Mascarpone is an incredibly light cream cheese made mostly in the Lombardy region of Italy. You may have trouble finding it, and if you are offered *torte*, which is Mascarpone layered with sweet Gorgonzola, be sure to accept it, because it is delicious in this dish, even if a slightly different flavor. If you can't get either imported cheese, use a good domestic cream cheese.

Penne al Salmone *("PEN" MACARONI WITH SMOKED SALMON)*   Serves 6

If you're fond of smoked salmon, this unusual Florentine pasta recipe makes a delightful first course, or a nice brunch dish. Since the smoked salmon is chopped for the sauce, you may be able to buy it in scraps or trimmings at less cost than the whole slices.
   Wine suggested: A Pinot Blanc or a Pinot Grigio.

3 tablespoons unsalted butter
3 ounces best-cure smoked salmon
   (mild salt and smoke),
   chopped finely
1 tablespoon finely chopped shallots
Juice of ½ large lemon
½ pint heavy cream
2 ounces Scotch whisky
Salt to taste
White pepper, a good amount
12 ounces dried pen macaroni
Freshly ground black pepper

Place the butter in a large frying pan over a low flame. When it has melted, add the salmon and shallot and cook for about 2 minutes. Then add the lemon juice and mix well. Add the cream and whisky and cook long enough to let the alcohol evaporate. Adjust salt and pepper. Mix well.

Meanwhile, cook the pasta *very* al dente (see page 24). Drain and add it, well dried, to the salmon mixture in the large frying pan. Gently mix so that the pasta is well coated. The sauce will finish cooking the pasta. Test for doneness. If the sauce is too dry, add some more cream. It should be very smooth and creamy, but the pasta should not swim in it. Fresh black pepper atop each serving "finishes" this dish.

Pasta Ericina *(PASTA AS MADE IN ERICE, SICILY)*   Serves 3 or 4

Erice is perched on top of a mountain high above the city of Trapani on the southwest coast of Sicily. It is one of the most beautiful sites in Italy, and with just a touch of imagination on a very clear day you can see the north coast of Africa from this picturesque ancient hill town.
   Wine suggested: A Zinfandel or a red Corvo.

1½ pounds skinned tomatoes, sun-
   ripe fresh, or canned
3 tablespoons olive oil, best quality
Salt and pepper to taste
6 leaves fresh basil, chopped,
   or 1 teaspoon dried
½ pound fresh pasta, fettucine cut;
   or dried spaghetti or penne
⅓ cup finely chopped fresh parsley
1 tablespoon finely chopped garlic

Puree the tomatoes and add a little olive oil. Add salt and pepper to taste and the basil. Let the mixture stand at room temperature for at least 1 hour to blend well.

Cook the pasta al dente (see page 24) and drain well. Add some of the tomato sauce, mix well, and add the rest. Place the pasta on a hot serving dish and add the chopped parsley all over the top. Then sprinkle on the garlic.

NOTE: The fresh Erice sauce can be used and served at room temperature; or it can be very gently heated. It should *not* be boiled or cooked. Depending upon the quality of your tomatoes, you will probably want to enjoy this dish "neat," with only the fresh flavors of the ingredients. If you wanted to, however, you could pass a little grated Parmesan or Romano cheese – freshly grated, please!

Trenette con Pesto *(PASTA WITH PESTO SAUCE)* *Serves 6*

This is always a favorite. The pesto's beautiful green color, its heady aroma and its exquisite flavor add up to a real taste treat. Followed by a breaded veal cutlet, a green salad and some fresh fruit with cheese, this can be a memorable meal.

Wine suggested: A Barbera or a Chianti Riserva.

1 cup Pesto Sauce (see page 32)
1 pound trenette pasta
¼ cup olive oil
Salt and pepper to taste
½ cup freshly grated Parmesan

Have the pesto at room temperature. Cook the pasta al dente (see page 24). Drain, but reserve about ¼ cup of the water to dilute the pesto a bit. Place the pasta in a warm bowl. Add the olive oil and toss well. Add the pesto, diluted with the pasta water, and toss again. Add salt and pepper to taste. Pass the grated Parmesan cheese separately.

Pasta alla Sciacquina *(PASTA WASHERWOMAN-STYLE)* *Serves 4*

This pasta with the humble name is actually quite elegant and fit for a king. The cream, prosciutto and best imported Parmesan are not inexpensive these days. They combine here to achieve an absolutely irresistible result.

Wine suggested: A Cabernet Sauvignon or a Chianti Riserva.

2½ cups Salsa al Pomodoro (Quick
**   Tomato Sauce, see page 31)**
½ cup heavy cream
¼ pound prosciutto, chopped finely
12 ounces fresh spaghetti,
**   or other long pasta**
Salt and pepper to taste
⅓ cup finely chopped fresh parsley
Grated Parmesan cheese to pass

Puree the prepared tomato sauce and add the heavy cream and prosciutto. Heat gently for about 10 minutes.

Cook the pasta al dente (see page 24). When done, drain well and put into a warm serving dish. Add some sauce and toss. Add more sauce and then sprinkle on the parsley. Finally, sprinkle grated cheese on top when the pasta is served up in individual dishes.

Maccheroni ai Quattro Formaggi
(MACARONI WITH FOUR CHEESES)   *Serves 6*

This is a rich and luxurious pasta, due to the abbondanza *(abundance) of beautiful cheeses used in the sauce. It is a good conversation piece and a lot of fun, making an important first course for a special-occasion menu. Be sure to follow it with a light and exquisite entree, such as veal scaloppine, squab, rack of lamb or game.*

Wine suggested: A Chablis or a Soave.

4 ounces unsalted butter
½ cup cream
⅓ cup shredded Gorgonzola cheese
⅓ cup shredded Fontina cheese
**⅓ cup shredded Gruyere or
  Emmenthaler cheese**
⅓ cup finely diced mozzarella cheese
**1 pound of any dried macaroni,
  such as rigatoni, penne, chiocciole
  or other fancy shape**
Salt and pepper to taste
**½ cup freshly grated
  Parmesan cheese**

Heat the butter and cream in a large saucepan, being careful to keep it from boiling. Whisk in the four shredded soft cheeses. Maintain the heat until they melt, well-whisked and blended. Remove from flame and set aside.

Meanwhile, cook the macaroni al dente (see page 24). Drain it and put it into a warm bowl. Pour over the thick melted cheese sauce and toss well. Add salt and pepper to taste.

Serve this dish piping hot and pass the freshly grated Parmesan at the table.

Pasta alla Norma *(PASTA WITH FRIED EGGPLANT)* *Serves 4 to 6*

This pasta is one of the gems in the crown of Sicilian cooking. Eaten outdoors with a soft Mediterranean breeze blowing, it will transport you to temporary heaven. The dish is known variously as Pasta con Melanzane *(eggplant),* Pasta alla Norma *(the opera), or* Pasta alla Bellini, *after the great Sicilian composer who wrote the opera.*

Wine suggested: A Zinfandel or a red Corvo.

1 quart Salsa al Pomodoro (Quick
    Tomato Sauce, see page 31)
1 large eggplant, plump and fresh
½ cup olive oil
Salt and pepper
1 pound fresh spaghetti, or about
    12 ounces of dried "strings"
    or rigatoni or penne
Several leaves fresh basil,
    chopped medium fine
½ cup freshly grated Ricotta Salata
    or Romano cheese

Prepare the tomato sauce and set it aside. Slice the eggplant lengthwise ¼ inch thick. Do not remove the skin. If it is truly fresh, there is no need to salt, weight and "leach" it, because the juice will not be bitter.

Fry the eggplant slices in hot olive oil, and after they are nicely browned, remove them from the frying pan to a dish lined with paper towels. Sprinkle with salt and freshly ground pepper. Set aside.

Cook the pasta al dente (see page 24). Drain it and put it in a warm bowl. Add a little of the sauce and toss. Serve on warm plates. Spoon a good amount of sauce on top of each portion and carefully lay 1 or 2 slices of fried eggplant on top of or alongside the sauce. Throw about a teaspoon of chopped fresh basil on top of each serving, and pass the cheese at the table.

NOTE: If fresh basil is not available, add a few teaspoons of dried basil to the tomato sauce before heating. Unless the oil is *very* hot (though it should not be smoking and burning) before you start to fry the eggplant, the slices will absorb and take up the oil and become soggy. To avoid this, fry the slices as quickly as possible in good, preheated oil, taking care that they don't burn.

Fettucine alla Romana
(RIBBON PASTA WITH CREAM, BUTTER AND CHEESE)

Serves 6

This pasta has become popularly known as "Fettucine Alfredo" after the Alfredo Restaurant in Rome. Alfredo "introduced" this dish to America at the 1939 World's Fair in New York, where he complained that he should have brought along some water from the aqueducts in Rome to make the dish really perfect. Until very recently Roman water was considered by many to be without peer.

Wine suggested: A Chablis or a Soave.

6 ounces best-quality unsalted butter
1½ cups heavy cream
6 ounces Parmesan cheese,
freshly grated
1 pound fresh pasta
A grating of fresh nutmeg, or a
good pinch of dried
Freshly ground pepper,
black or white

Soften the butter to room temperature. Place it in a large, heavy frying pan or similar vessel and put it in a very warm place, even over very low heat, to melt but not cook. Warm your serving dishes. Bring the cream to room temperature or warmer, and keep it handy, as well as the cheese.

Cook the pasta al dente (see page 24). Quickly drain it, but don't shake all the water out, just most of it.

Immediately put the drained pasta into the frying pan with the butter and toss all around to coat the pasta well. Add the heavy cream and then the grated cheese and gently toss it all around again. Add some nutmeg and the ground pepper and serve the pasta, which should be eaten immediately. Pass more cheese at the table.

NOTES: If the pasta looks a little too wet, don't worry. The pasta, as it sits in the dish, will take up quite a bit of the liquid. If the pasta looks perfectly creamy when you first serve it, it may become dry on the plate. Just to be sure, you may want to serve some additional soft unsalted butter along with additional cheese.

• Also, you can partially whip the cream for the sauce so that it resembles a genuine "double cream" such as you would find in England. This increases the volume of the cream, but it also makes it lighter and more airy. It is a good idea, and you should try it at least once. Another name for the dish in Italy is *Tagliatelle alla Panna, panna* meaning cream.

• The amounts given in this recipe are only a guide to quantities. I have never really measured when making this dish personally and I would find it offensive to have to do so. The result you will get is a matter of judgment refined by experience and taste.

Linguine alle Vongole *(PASTA WITH CLAMS)* *Serves 4*

This is a deservedly popular dish. It is quick and easy to make, at least with canned clams, which are available to most people. It can make a satisfying meal along with a green salad, a piece of fruit and some good coffee.

Wine suggested: A Pinot Blanc or a Verdicchio.

**3 pounds small clams in their shells,
  or 2 7-ounce cans of chopped clams
  in their juice**
⅓ cup olive oil
**2 or 3 large garlic cloves,
  finely chopped**
Salt to taste
Plenty of freshly ground black pepper
2 tablespoons chopped parsley
**1 pound pasta, fresh or dried –
  linguine, spaghetti or similar
  long shape**
**Optional, but really good: A good
  pinch of crushed red chili peppers,
  or ⅓ cup heavy cream**

Wash the clam shells well, scrubbing them with a brush to remove sand and debris. Place them in a big frying pan with a little olive oil. Cover the pan and cook on a fast flame until the shells open wide. You may serve the clams in their shells, or remove the clams from their shells at this point and discard the shells. Either way, set aside. Then, strain the pan juices through a fine sieve to eliminate additional bits of shell and sand. Reserve the liquid.

Put the olive oil in a frying pan and add the garlic. Brown well but *do not burn!* Add the clam juice, salt and pepper and one of the options, if desired. Add the parsley and the fresh or canned clams. Remove from heat; set aside.

Meanwhile cook the pasta al dente (see page 24). When it is done, drain it well. Then pour the hot clam sauce over it (reheating the sauce first, if necessary). Mix the pasta well with the sauce and serve at once. Do *not* serve cheese with this dish.

Bucatini all'Amatriciana
(MACARONI WITH BACON AND TOMATO)

Serves 6

This dish comes from the town of Amatrice on the east coast of Italy by the Adriatic Sea. It has been adopted by the Romans, however, who have made the dish their own by adding some hot red pepper flakes, and also by sometimes using smaller cuts of pasta such as spaghetti in the recipe. Try the dish with and without the pepper flakes, and with larger and smaller pastas, and choose the version you like best.

Wine suggested: A bold red wine such as Zinfandel would be good; or you can try a Valpolicella.

2 tablespoons olive oil
6 ounces pancetta, diced small or sliced very thinly
1 small onion, finely chopped
5 or 6 small fresh tomatoes, peeled, seeded and diced; or use the canned equivalent
Salt to taste
Freshly ground black pepper
1 pound bucatini or perciatelle dried pasta
A good pinch of red pepper flakes
½ cup freshly grated Pecorino or Romano cheese

Heat the oil in a frying pan. Add the pancetta and onion and cook until light gold in color. Add the chopped tomatoes and cook gently, but do not let them get too soft. The pieces should remain intact. Taste and adjust the salt and pepper.

Cook the pasta al dente (see page 24). Drain and place it in a warm bowl. Add the sauce and toss well. Adjust again for salt and pepper, and add the red pepper flakes and the cheese. Toss once more and serve hot, passing additional cheese at the table.

Spaghetti alla Carbonara
(SPAGHETTI COAL-VENDORS' STYLE)

Serves 4 to 6

Some say this is a relatively new pasta recipe, originating after World War II in Rome when the Allied troops restored the city's supplies of eggs and bacon. Others say the dish has been used around the Sicilian coal mines since ancient times. I subscribe to the latter belief.

If you offer a simple antipasto (such as tuna fish in olive oil, Italian olives, celery and mildly hot pepperoncini), accompany the Spaghetti alla Carbonara with a nice big spinach salad and follow with fresh fruit in season, you can serve a delicious meal with almost no labor at all.

Wine suggested: A Zinfandel or a Montepulciano d'Abbruzzo.

2 tablespoons olive oil
4 medium-size garlic cloves, slightly crushed
⅓ to ½ pound pancetta
Generous ¼ cup dry white wine
4 large eggs, slightly beaten
Generous amount freshly ground black pepper
Salt to taste
2 tablespoons finely chopped parsley
1 pound fresh or dried pasta
½ cup or more freshly grated cheese, Romano or Parmesan, or both

Put the oil and garlic in a frying pan and cook over medium heat until the garlic is golden. Discard the garlic.

Add the pancetta to the pan and cook until it is a light golden color. Do not let it burn.

Add the wine and let it boil for 3 or 4 minutes. Turn off the heat and set the pan inside.

In the bowl from which you will serve the pasta place the beaten eggs, black pepper, all of the cheese and the parsley. Mix together well with a fork, so that the ingredients are well blended. Set the bowl aside in a warm spot—*not* in a hot spot like the oven, or you will cook the eggs. The eggs should not cook; they simply coat the pasta and make a delicious sauce.

Cook the pasta al dente (see page 24). Drain it well and then add it to the eggs in the bowl, stirring vigorously all the while so that the eggs will cover the hot pasta without scrambling. In the meantime, reheat the pancetta until it is piping hot. Add it to the pasta mixture and toss well again. Serve immediately and pass more grated cheese at the table, if you wish.

NOTE: There is a great debate as to whether to use American-style smoked bacon or the Italian salt-cured pancetta. In Rome you can get the dish either way, depending on who is making it. Try it both ways. I prefer the pancetta. Some people add 3 or 4 tablespoons of heavy cream to the sauce. This is entirely optional. I don't feel the dish needs it, so I don't use it myself.

Bigoli all'Anitra *(VENETIAN WHEAT PASTA WITH POACHED DUCK)* Serves 8

This is an unusual dish—though not in Venice—that you will really enjoy. Duck is most often served roasted and, while it is delicious that way, this recipe presents an interesting alternative. You can either make the Bigoli whole wheat pasta fresh, following the recipe on page 18, or purchase dried whole wheat commercial pasta at a health food store.

Wine suggested: This dish is good with either red or white wine. I would prefer a red wine such as a burgundy or a Barbera d'Asti, or a nice white such as a Pinot Grigio from the Veneto region around Venice, the home of this recipe.

THE DUCK:

4-pound duckling, cleaned and ready to cook (reserve the duck liver)
1 large yellow onion, coarsely chopped
1 branch celery, coarsely chopped
1 large carrot, coarsely chopped
Salt to taste

THE SAUCE:

6-8 tablespoons butter
1 large onion, finely chopped
1 branch celery, finely chopped
1 large carrot, diced small
4 fresh sage leaves, chopped, or 2 teaspoons dried
Duck liver, cut in 1-inch pieces
Poached duck meat, diced
Salt and pepper to taste
1 pound bigoli whole wheat pasta
⅔ cup freshly grated Parmesan cheese

Put the duckling whole into a stock pot, together with the chopped onion, celery and carrot. (Don't use too large a pot.) Cover with cold water half again as high as the duck. Add salt.

Bring the pot to a slow simmer. Skim the fat and scum from the surface of the water from time to time. Cook until the duck is tender, about 1 to 1½ hours. (If you are making the bigoli pasta fresh, this is the time to do it.)

When the duck is done, remove the carcass and skin it. (Save the skin and fry it in a little butter. When crisp it is delicious added to a salad or just eaten by itself.) Remove the duck meat in small chunks. Set aside to cool; then chop into dice. Strain the broth and degrease it. Discard the vegetables and reserve the broth.

To make the sauce, melt the butter in a frying pan. Add the chopped onion, carrot and celery and cook until golden. Add the sage and stir well. Add the duck liver (add *more* duck livers if you can get extras!) and cook for about 3 minutes. Then add the diced duck meat and salt and pepper to taste. Cook until everything is hot.

Cook the pasta al dente (see page 24), using the reserved duck broth instead of water. Drain when done, again reserving the duck broth. Add the sauce to the drained pasta and mix well. Sprinkle on half of the cheese and serve hot. Pass the remaining cheese at the table.

NOTE: This is obviously a good main-dish pasta, if not a whole meal. There are also the added dividends of the rich duck broth and skin for many other uses later on.

Paglia e Fieno *(STRAW AND HAY PASTA)*

This is one of the times that I believe spinach pasta is well justified. The color contrast in this dish is lovely, and the flavor is so good that it puts the recipe in a class by itself. Obviously one can see how its name came about. The charm wore thin, however, when I was researching the origins of the recipe to check for authenticity. In true Italian fashion I can point to at least five "proper" ways of preparing this dish, each one so different from the other that it is impossible to see how they can all refer to the same pasta. But at least they all do agree on its colors.

Wine suggested: A Pinot Blanc or a Verdicchio.

4 tablespoons butter
1 medium-size yellow onion, finely diced
8 ounces boiled ham, shredded; or 5 ounces prosciutto, shredded
⅔ cup fresh tiny peas, or frozen tiny peas
1 cup heavy cream
Salt and pepper to taste
2 generous gratings fresh nutmeg
½ pound plain tagliarini (tagliolini)
½ pound green spinach pasta, same cut
¾ cup freshly grated Parmesan cheese

Melt the butter in a heavy frying pan. Add the onion and cook until transparent.

Add the ham and prosciutto and cook for about 5 minutes.

Add the peas and stir well for about 1 minute.

Add the cream and cook for another 5 minutes to allow the cream to thicken a little. Then add the salt and pepper to taste, and the nutmeg.

Meanwhile cook the pasta al dente (see page 24).

The making of spinach pasta is described on page 18, or you can buy it dried. Whether you use fresh or dried pasta, remember that spinach pasta will cook faster than the plain kind, so put the plain pasta in the water for about a minute before you add the spinach pasta in order to equalize cooking times. Also, both pastas should be as close to each other in type or formula as possible, whether dried or fresh.

When done, drain the pasta and put it in a warm bowl. Add half the sauce and half the cheese and mix very well. Add the remaining sauce on top and the remaining cheese. Pass more cheese separately if you wish.

Spaghetti alla Puttanesca *(HOOKERS' PASTA)*

Serves 4 or 6

No one seems to know why this pasta should be named after the ladies in the world's oldest profession. Perhaps the fact that it can be eaten cold may mean that they could cook, do some business and then have a tasty cold meal ready. I'm afraid I don't know, but the dish is quite good!

Wine suggested: A Pinot Noir or a Barbaresco.

2 or 3 tablespoons olive oil
2 garlic cloves, minced
2 ounces or more Calamata black olives, pitted and coarsely chopped
1 teaspoon coarsely chopped capers
1 large fresh tomato, peeled and coarsely chopped
4 or 5 anchovy fillets, coarsely chopped
1 pound spaghetti
⅓ cup finely chopped parsley
Salt and pepper to taste

Place the olive oil in a frying pan and add the minced garlic. When it is golden, add the olives, capers, tomatoes and anchovy fillets. Stir well and heat through for about 6 minutes.

Cook the pasta al dente (see page 24) and drain it. Place it in a warm bowl and add half of the sauce. Toss well. Add the remaining sauce and sprinkle on the parsley with some salt and pepper to taste. Serve hot.

There is no cheese used with this dish, and it can also be eaten later cold.

Spaghetti alla Viareggina
(SPAGHETTI WITH CLAMS AND TOMATO)

Serves 4 to 6

This very popular dish from Viareggio in Tuscany is equally at home in Rome, Naples and Sicily. It is often made with linguine and other long pastas. Even people who do not ordinarily care much for clams will eat this recipe with gusto. There is a very fresh quality about this pasta that makes you want to eat something more, even though you may already be quite full. A nice small breaded veal cutlet just plain, with a splash of lemon juice, is a perfect follow-up.

Wine suggested: A good young wine of the Beaujolais type or a Bardolino would be my choice with this pasta, whether I planned to have veal afterwards, or not.

⅓ cup olive oil
3 large garlic cloves, finely chopped
⅓ cup white wine
1 pound fresh tomatoes, peeled and
   chopped; or use canned tomatoes
3 pounds small clams in their
   shells, or 2 7-ounce cans of
   chopped clams in their juice
Salt to taste
Plenty of freshly ground
   black pepper
Generous pinch red chili
   pepper flakes
1 pound spaghetti
⅓ cup chopped parsley

Wash and prepare clams (see Linguine alle Vongole, page 43).

Put the olive oil in a frying pan and add the garlic. Brown well, but *do not burn.*

Add the tomatoes, clams and their juice and taste for salt. Correct as needed. Cook all together over high heat for 2 minutes. Add black pepper and red chili pepper and cook until the clams are done and the sauce is slightly thickened. Do not overcook the clams.

Meanwhile cook the spaghetti al dente (see page 24). Drain well and place in a warm bowl. Add half the sauce and mix well. Add the remaining sauce on top and sprinkle on the chopped parsley. Please, no cheese with this dish.

Maccheroni con la Capuliata *(MACARONI WITH GROUND MEAT)* Serves 4

Capuliata is Sicilian dialect for chopped beef, which is quite a treat for Sicilians. Because they are poor, their consumption runs more to fish, game, pork, kid and chicken. This is a hearty dish, satisfying to both soul and body; it makes a wonderful one-dish supper.

Wine suggested: A robust red wine such as a Cabernet Sauvignon or a Valpolicella.

¼ cup olive oil
1 onion, finely chopped
1 large garlic clove, finely chopped
½ pound, or a little more, ground beef,
   preferably chuck
½ cup red wine
3 tablespoons chopped parsley
2 tablespoons chopped fresh basil
   leaves, or 3 tablespoons dried
1 pound fresh tomatoes, peeled and
   finely chopped, or 1 pound canned
Salt and pepper to taste
1 pinch red pepper flakes
12 ounces dried pasta, short stubby
   shape, such as penne or rigatoni
¾ cup grated Provolone or
   Cacciocavallo cheese

Heat the oil and gently cook the onion until just soft. Add the garlic and cook until golden.

Add the meat and cook it, stirring to break up any lumps, until it just loses its redness.

Add the wine and cook for about 10 minutes more.

Add everything else except the pasta and the grated cheese. Simmer the mixture together for about 30 minutes.

Cook the pasta al dente (see page 24). Drain it, place it in a bowl and mix it with half of the sauce and half of the cheese. Pour on the rest of the sauce and the rest of the cheese. Serve it very hot and pass extra cheese at the table if you wish.

NOTE: In Sicily this dish is often prepared as described and, when completed, put into a well-oiled casserole. The top is sprinkled liberally with more cheese, and the dish is then baked in a preheated 400-degree oven for about 20 minutes. It is served very hot.

Rigatoni Donnafugata

This is my own version of a very enjoyable pasta featured at the Fico D'India Restaurant in Palermo, Sicily. Literally translated, donnafugata *means, in Arabic, "enclosed fountain," though in Italian it means "woman fled." It is the name given by Giuseppe di Lampedusa in his book,* The Leopard, *to the beloved country palace of Don Fabrizio, Prince of Salina. The novel, set in the mid-19th century, portrays the opulent life of the nobility of the era before Garibaldi unified Italy. This complex and sumptuous recipe could well be used today as a main-dish pasta.*

Wine suggested: A Pinot Noir or a Barbera.

½ pound veal shoulder, or
   leftover cooked veal
1 cup veal or chicken broth
3 sprigs of parsley
1 small carrot
1 bay leaf
¼ cup olive oil
¼ cup pancetta, finely chopped
4-6 scallions, finely chopped
¼ pound prosciutto,
   medium chopped
14 artichoke hearts, trimmed,
   blanched and quartered, or
   10-ounce package of frozen
   artichoke hearts, quartered
3-4 tablespoons tomato paste
¼ cup or a little more Marsala
Salt and pepper to taste
¼ pound fresh mushrooms,
   thinly sliced
1 cup fresh or frozen tiny peas
1½ cups heavy cream
1¼ pounds dried rigatoni
2 tablespoons butter
Parmesan cheese, freshly grated

Cut the veal into small pieces about 2 inches square. Cook it in chicken or veal broth with parsley, carrot and bay leaf until tender, about 1 hour. Drain the meat, shred it and set it aside. Strain the broth and reserve it.

Heat the oil in a heavy frying pan. Add the chopped pancetta and cook it until it is slightly colored. Add the chopped scallions, prosciutto, veal and artichokes. Cook for about 7 or 8 minutes. Add the tomato paste, Marsala, broth, salt and pepper, and simmer for 7 or 8 minutes. Add the mushrooms and peas to the sauce mixture and simmer for 5 minutes. Add the heavy cream and continue to cook until all ingredients are very hot and the cream is heated through.

Meantime, cook the pasta al dente (see page 24). Drain it, return it to the pot and toss quickly with a shot of oil or butter.

Place the pasta in a bowl and top with the sauce. Serve the dish hot at once, and pass grated Parmesan cheese at the table.

50 / PASTA! COOKING IT, LOVING IT

Pasta Arriminata *(PASTA WITH BROCCOLI "STIRRED AROUND")* *Serves 6*

This dish is representative of the ingenious flavors and textures of the Sicilian cuisine, which is certainly the most complex of all the Italian local cuisines and the hardest to understand. However, if you simply let yourself enjoy the tastes without worrying about analyzing them, you will find this dish, along with so many other Sicilian dishes, a rewarding experience.

Wine suggested: A Grey Riesling or a white Corvo.

1 **bunch broccoli, trimmed and cut into pieces about 1½ inches square (cauliflower may be used instead)**
⅓ **cup olive oil**
1 **large yellow onion, cut in small dice**
3 **anchovy fillets, chopped**
½ **cup seedless white raisins**
⅓ **cup pine nuts**
Small pinch saffron
Salt and pepper to taste
1 **pound dried macaroni, such as rigatoni, penne, large shells or large elbows**
½ **cup or more freshly grated Pecorino cheese**

Blanch the broccoli or cauliflower in boiling salted water until it is barely tender. Do not overcook. Drain, cool and set aside.

Heat the oil in a frying pan. Fry the onion to a golden color. Add the broccoli or cauliflower, anchovy fillets, raisins, pine nuts, pinch of saffron and salt and pepper to taste. Gently cook until all is well flavored, about 5 or 6 minutes.

Meanwhile boil the pasta al dente (see page 24). Drain it when done, but leave about ¼ cup of water in the pasta. Add the sauce and stir well. Sprinkle on the Pecorino. Serve hot.

NOTE: Sometimes this dish will have about 1 cup crushed tomatoes added to the sauce during cooking. Also, it is sometimes put into a 400-degree oven in an oiled casserole for 20 minutes before serving.

Stuffed Pasta

(Pasta Ripieni)

Tortellini *(STUFFED RINGS OF PASTA)*

Makes about 300

These nuggets of sheer delight are loved by everyone who eats them in their many sauces and in Brodo (broth). Mention a soup in Bologna, where these are made, and you will immediately hear Tortellini in Brodo. About 18 tortellini per person are served with soup, and about 24 per person with sauce.

Wine suggested: A Chianti Classico Riserva would be excellent.

A 4-egg pasta dough (see page 13)
2 tablespoons unsalted butter
4 ounces lean pork, finely ground
4 ounces veal, finely ground
2 ounces chicken breast,
   finely ground
1 ounce mortadella, finely ground
2 slices prosciutto, finely ground
½ pound fresh ricotta
½ cup grated Parmesan cheese
1 egg, beaten
Scant ½ teaspoon (or 1 generous
   grating) of nutmeg
Salt and pepper to taste

Prepare the pasta dough as directed. Set it aside to rest.

Melt the butter in a frying pan over very low heat. Add the pork and cook for about 2 minutes. Then add the veal and chicken and cook for 7 or 8 minutes more. Set aside to cool completely; cold is even better. Add all the other ingredients and mix very well. Taste and adjust seasonings; the flavors should be pronounced because you will be using tiny amounts.

Roll out the pasta in thin sheets. Do *not* dry. Work with one sheet at a time, keeping the remaining dough wrapped in plastic film or foil. This pasta should be very soft.

With a cookie cutter or a glass, stamp out circles of pasta that are 2 inches in diameter. Put a ¼ teaspoon of filling in the center of each pasta circle, and fold it in half like a

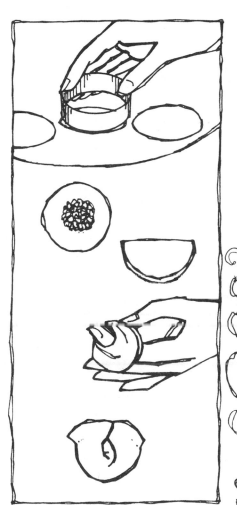

turnover, except that the bottom edge should fall below the top edge when folded (if the edge is double the pasta rings will be too thick). Press the bottom edge down firmly so that it will stick and not come apart.

Take the two points of the long straight side of the half circle, wrap them around your finger, and overlap and press the ends to seal. While wrapping, at the same time push the curved side up toward the end of your finger. If your fingers aren't too big, you will produce a stuffed pasta ring.

Tortellini can be cooked in a rich homemade chicken or veal broth, if you have it, and served as a first course with a spoonful of grated Parmesan. Heavenly!

NOTE: Tortellini are delicious in a Balsamella sauce with a little Parmesan; with melted butter and grated cheese; with tomato sauce and cheese; and they can be made even tastier by putting them into a hot 400-degree oven for 10 or 12 minutes to get a little brown at the edges.

CAPPELLETTI (little hats)

These are made in the same way as tortellini, except that the pasta cuts will be 1½ inches square instead of round. After you have filled them, fold in small triangles with the top edge below the bottom edge. Wrap and press around your finger, and the tip of the triangle sticking up is supposed to resemble a bishop's miter. Have fun with both shapes!

Ravioli *(STUFFED PASTA PILLOWS)*

The fillings for Ravioli are as varied as the people who make them. The word comes from the Genovese robiole *meaning rubbish, or in our case, leftovers. Use your imagination and make your own ravioli dish. It is very difficult to make a "real" ravioli stuffing because it is so often determined by what is at hand. For instance, you may substitute the same quantity (and quality) of ground chicken and veal for the meats used in this recipe. All kinds of rollers, molds and forms are available to help you shape and seal the ravioli. If you plan to make them frequently, you may find one of these useful.*

Wine suggested: A Cabernet Sauvignon or Vino Nobile di Montepulciano.

A 3-egg pasta dough (see page 13)
2 tablespoons olive oil
1 cup ground beef
1 cup ground pork
2 ounces prosciutto or mortadella, ground
½ cup best-quality boiled ham, ground
1 garlic clove, minced
2 generous gratings fresh nutmeg
½ cup freshly grated Parmesan cheese
Salt and pepper
2 whole eggs
½ recipe, or 1 quart Salsa al Pomodoro (Quick Tomato Sauce, see page 31)

Prepare the dough as directed. Set it aside to rest.

Heat the oil and gently cook the meat until it loses its red color (unless you are using already cooked leftover meat). Set it aside to cool.

When cool, combine the next 7 ingredients and blend them well into a smooth paste.

Roll out the pasta dough to about ⅛ inch or a bit thinner. Do *not* dry it, because for stuffed pasta you *do* want it to stick to itself. You will need 2 broad sheets of pasta to make each sheet of ravioli.

Place the filling, 1 tablespoon at a time, in even rows across and down 1 sheet of pasta, leaving about 1½ inches between each mound. Place another sheet of pasta on top, and press it down well with your fingers between the mounds of filling in lines to form the ravioli squares. Cut out the squares on the pressed lines with a crimped pastry cutter. Set the ravioli aside to rest on a floured cloth. Be careful not to pile them on top of each other or they will stick.

Just before serving, boil the ravioli as directed on page 24. Drain them and lay them on a warm dish. Pour the sauce on top and serve hot, passing more grated Parmesan cheese at the table.

Agnolotti *(ROUND STUFFED PASTA "LAMBS")*

Agnolotti *(little lambs), in case you haven't guessed, are ravioli in sheep's clothing. So many Italian names are whimsical and express someone's imagination that they add to the maddening confusion of trying to identify and codify Italian dishes. Thank heaven they are so delicious! An error in name will still get you a gastronomic treat.*

Wine suggested: A light red wine such as a Beaujolais or the Sicilian Corvo is very good with this dish because the flavors of the dish are smooth, as are the flavors of this type of wine.

A 3-egg pasta dough (see page 13)
2 bunches spinach, well washed
8 tablespoons butter
1 small yellow onion, finely diced
½ pound ground beef
1 slice mortadella, finely chopped
Salt and pepper to taste
½ cup freshly grated
  Parmesan cheese
½ recipe, or 1 quart Salsa
  di Pomodoro Stracotto
  (Slow Tomato Sauce, see page 30)

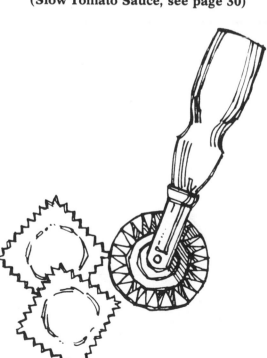

Prepare the dough as directed. Set it aside to rest.

Shake the excess water from the spinach and steam it in a covered pot, using only the water left on the leaves. When it has just "collapsed," remove the lid and let it dry out a bit over low heat. Set it aside to cool.

Melt the butter in a frying pan. Cook the onions just until they are transparent. Add the beef and cook just until it loses its red color. Set aside to cool.

Combine the mortadella, ¼ cup of the Parmesan cheese and salt and pepper to taste. Add the mixture to the cooled spinach and meat; blend well.

Roll out the pasta dough to about ⅛ inch or a little thinner. Do *not* dry it! You will need 2 broad sheets of pasta to make each sheet of filled pasta shapes.

Place the filling, 1 tablespoon at a time, in even rows across and down 1 sheet of pasta, leaving about 1½ inches between mounds. Cover with another sheet of pasta and press down with your fingers all around each mound of filling in a circular shape. Then cut out the circles through the pressed part with a shot glass, a cookie cutter or a special agnolotti cutter. Set the pastas to rest on a floured cloth. Make sure they don't touch each other or they will stick.

Just before serving, boil the agnolotti in plenty of salted water for about 5 minutes (see page 24); meanwhile heat the sauce. Drain the pastas, place them on a warm dish and cover with sauce. Pass the remaining grated Parmesan cheese at the table.

NOTE: If you have any trouble getting any of the stuffed pastas to stick together and hold in the filling, you can use an egg wash (beaten raw egg applied with a pastry brush) as your "glue."

Conchiglie Ripieni *(STUFFED PASTA SHELLS)*   *Allow 2 or 3 per serving*

This is an excellent dish for entertaining as it can be prepared ready for the oven in advance, even frozen, and heated just before serving. A nice variation is to make two fillings, one with meat and the other with ricotta and spinach, and serve both types.
   Wine suggested: A Pinot Noir or a Chianti Riserva.

**1 quart Balsamella
(White Sauce, see page 34)
1 pint Salsa al Pomodoro
(Quick Tomato Sauce, see page 31)
Pasta shells, commercial dried,
   jumbo size
2 pounds ricotta
¼ pound prosciutto, finely minced
1 cup mozzarella or jack cheese,
   finely diced
¼ cup finely chopped fresh parsley
2 eggs
Salt and pepper to taste
½ cup grated Parmesan or
   Romano cheese**

Prepare your ovenproof casserole dishes by spreading an ⅛-inch layer of white sauce on the bottoms. Set them aside.

Mix the ricotta, prosciutto, mozzarella, parsley and eggs together in a bowl. Adjust salt and pepper. Set aside.

Cook the pasta shells according to the directions on the package, but undercook them by about 1½ minutes (*very* al dente). Drain the shells and plunge them into cold water for a minute to stop the cooking process. Drain again and place them on an oiled tray.

Fill the shells with the ricotta mixture, using a pastry tube for convenience. A spoon or knife will work, but that method is very slow. Place the filled shells on the bed of white sauce on the bottom of the prepared casseroles, arranging them fairly close together, but not too tightly packed.

Put some more white sauce on top of the shells in the casseroles, and then drizzle some tomato sauce over that. Sprinkle grated cheese on top.

When you are ready to serve, preheat the oven to 350 degrees. Cook the conchiglie for about 20 minutes. Serve very hot.

NOTE: You can assemble this dish totally and freeze it. However, it should not be thawed before heating, or the pasta will become soggy. Try to freeze it in a metal or unbreakable ovenproof dish and simply place it covered (and frozen) in a 350-degree oven for an hour before serving.

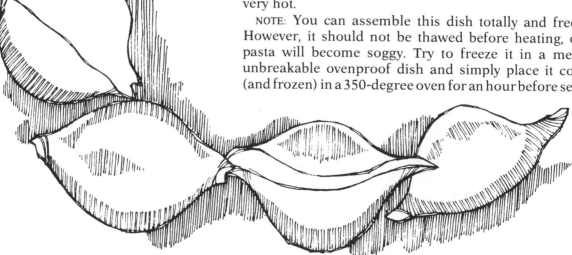

Cannelloni *(STUFFED LARGE REEDS)*

Cannelloni is one of the most ubiquitous and universal of all of the Italian "export" pasta dishes. It is sometimes made with a rolled crêpe or a light pancake for the casing instead of pasta, making it a first cousin to the wonderful crêpe dishes from the cuisines of Italy's neighbors to the north. Nonetheless, the basic fresh pasta cannellonis have a character all their own which can add a special style to almost any menu.

Wine suggested: A Dry Sémillon or a Pinot Bianco.

A 3-egg pasta dough (see page 13)
1 bunch spinach
  (or 1 package frozen)
1 medium-size yellow onion,
  finely chopped
2 tablespoons olive oil
½ pound ground beef or veal
½ cup finely chopped
  mortadella (or unsmoked ham)
2 generous gratings fresh nutmeg,
  to taste
¼ cup freshly grated
  Parmesan cheese
1 egg, beaten
1 recipe Salsa al Pomodoro
  (Quick Tomato Sauce, page 31)
1 recipe Balsamella
  (White Sauce, see page 34)

Prepare the dough as directed and set it aside to rest.

Cook the spinach, as little as possible. Drain it and chop it medium fine. Set aside.

Put the onion, oil, meat, and mortadella in a frying pan and cook until all are done. Add the spinach, nutmeg and cheese. Mix thoroughly and set aside to cool. Stir in the beaten egg, and you will have enough filling for 12 cannelloni.

Roll the pasta out in large sheets, not too thin. Cut it into rectangles about 4 by 5 inches. You can expect to get about 12 pieces from the 3-egg pasta dough, but this is not gospel. Find out for yourself. If you have more cannelloni, you can always make more filling.

Boil a large amount of water and add some salt to it. Drop in 2 or 3 pieces of pasta at a time and cook for about 2 minutes. Lift them out and plunge them in cold water to stop the cooking (remember they will cook more later). Lay them on damp towels to keep them moist.

Spread a generous row of filling down the long side of each rectangle and roll it up. Place the filled cannelloni in a well-buttered ovenproof baking dish. Arrange the "reeds" attractively in the dish and spread over them either or both sauces in a nice design. Put some grated cheese on top and bake in a 375-degree oven for about 20 minutes.

NOTE: Because they are finished in the oven, cannellonis can be prepared ahead up to adding the sauces, and can be held back for a while before baking and serving. They are wonderful for a hot buffet, brunch or lunch, and can also be made, of course, in individual small baking dishes. You can also substitute 1 pound of ricotta cheese for the meats as a variation; and, if you don't want to make the pasta casings, you can purchase commercial manicotti shells, fill them with a pastry tube and proceed as directed.

Pansoti con Salsa di Noce
(PASTA PILLOWS OF RICOTTA WITH WALNUT SAUCE)   *Serves 8*

This dish is worthy of a try. I would use it in a menu that included broiled or roasted meat or fowl. The bitter taste of the watercress is refreshing to the palate, and it makes a good foil for the walnut flavor. Wine suggested: A bold red wine such as Zinfandel, Pinot Noir or a Gattinara.

A 4-egg pasta dough (see page 13)

FILLING:
1 pound Swiss chard
1 bunch watercress (or borage)
2 whole eggs
⅔ cup ricotta
½ cup grated Parmesan cheese
2 generous gratings fresh nutmeg
Salt and pepper to taste

SAUCE:
½ pound walnut meats
3 tablespoons pine nuts
1 small garlic clove
3 tablespoons parsley
⅓ cup curdled milk (add a few
   drops of lemon juice to warmed
   milk and let it stand at room
   temperature for a while)
½ cup olive oil

Prepare the dough as directed. Set aside to rest.

Wash the chard well in cold water. Shake out the excess water and steam the chard in a covered pan just until done—it should not be mushy. Drain it well.

Put the chard in a food processor, or chop it finely by hand. Add the watercress, raw eggs, ricotta, Parmesan, nutmeg and adjust salt and pepper. Blend well. If the mixture looks too wet or runny, add a little more grated Parmesan, or a tablespoon of breadcrumbs. Set aside.

Roll out the pasta dough as thin as possible, or less than 1/16th of an inch. Do *not* dry! It should be nice and moist so that it *will* stick on itself.

You will need 2 sheets of pasta to make each sheet of filled pansoti. You should divide your dough so as to have about 4 large sheets of pasta for this recipe.

Place the filling, 1 tablespoon at a time, in even rows across and down 1 sheet of pasta about 1½ inches apart. Lay another sheet of pasta on top and press with your fingers around each mound of filling to seal the dough. Pansoti's authentic shape is a triangle, but if this is too difficult, squares taste just as good. Cut out the filled pastas with a crimped pastry wheel and set them aside on a floured cloth, separated so they won't stick together. These can be made early in the day, or even frozen for later use.

Put the walnuts, pine nuts, garlic and parsley into the food processor and blend them into a smooth paste. Add the curdled milk and mix well; then the oil and blend some more. (This was originally made with a mortar and pestle, which takes longer, of course.)

Cook the pansoti in lots of boiling, salted water for about 5 minutes (if frozen, 1 minute longer). Do not overcook. Drain well and add sauce. Toss well and serve hot, passing more grated cheese at the table.

Tortelloni (Toscana) *(TORTELLONI AS MADE IN TUSCANY)*   Serves 4 to 6

This is an unusual and delicious stuffed pasta, which should only be made fresh. There is something quite tantalizing about the tender pasta dough, the slightly hot and piquant filling and the pungent sage butter sauce. The combination tempts one to fill up on this satisfying dish.
   Wine suggested: A Barbera or a Chianti Riserva.

A 3-egg pasta dough (see page 13)

FILLING:
8 ounces finely ground pork meat
   with some fat
3-4 tablespoons white wine
Salt and pepper to taste
1 large garlic clove, minced
3-4 tablespoons minced parsley
1-2 tablespoons tomato paste
¼ cup grated Pecorino cheese
3-4 tablespoons breadcrumbs
2 eggs
Big pinch crushed red pepper flakes

SAUCE:
16 tablespoons butter
8-10 fresh sage leaves, broken
   or torn in thirds

1 cup grated Parmesan cheese
Freshly ground black pepper

Prepare the dough as directed. Set aside to rest.

For the filling, cook the pork just until done. Add the white wine and cook for about 2 minutes more. Set aside to cool, and when cool, add the other filling ingredients and mix well.

Next, roll out the pasta in wide sheets about the same thickness as used for fettucine. Place mounds of the meat filling mixture, about 1 tablespoon each, in straight rows about 2½ inches apart. Cover with another sheet of pasta. Press the sheets together with your fingers between the mounds of filling. Cut with a crimped cutter into large squares about 2½ inches square. Keep the dough moist while working so it will stick together, or use a little whole beaten egg as "glue."

Cook the tortelloni in plenty of boiling salted water until just al dente (see page 24). Be very careful not to overcook or they will fall apart.

Meanwhile make the sauce. Melt the butter over *very low heat.* When melted, add the sage leaves and stir well. Keep hot.

Drain the tortelloni. Warm a serving dish and put a little of the sauce in the bottom of it. Add a layer of tortelloni, then sauce and grated cheese, and repeat until you end up with butter sauce and cheese on top of the dish. Grind some fresh black pepper on top and serve hot.

Baked Pasta

(Pasta al Forno)

Pasta al Forno (BAKED MACARONI)

Serves 8 to 12

This is a famous and traditional dish in Italy, particularly in and around Palermo in Sicily. It is a dish used for festive occasions when families gather together, Christmas being one of the most important. It is a wonderful dish for a large party, especially at a buffet, because it is plentiful and easy to serve. To me this dish is much like the wonderful madeleines *were to Marcel Proust in his memoirs. Boyhood memories leap forth when I eat Pasta al Forno, which was always made with such love by my family.*

Wine suggestion: Burgundy would be a good choice. The wonderful Italian red Corvo is perfect with this dish. Whichever red wine you choose should have some age and be quite robust.

1 recipe plus a little more Salsa di Pomodoro Stracotto (Slow Tomato Sauce, see page 30)
2 pounds beef rump or pork butt roast
Shortening for greasing casserole
½ cup breadcrumbs
4 hard-boiled eggs
1½ pounds best-quality commercial dried pasta, such as spaghetti, ruoti, mostaccioli, rigatoni, large or small, as you please

Prepare the sauce as directed, adding the meat in one solid piece. Cook slowly for up to 3 hours.

Prepare a 4-quart ovenproof casserole by spreading a moderate amount of shortening on its sides and bottom. Pour in the breadcrumbs and twist and turn the casserole until the sides and bottom are evenly coated. Gently shake out any excess. Set aside.

Remove the piece of meat from the sauce and let it cool to room temperature. Shred it with a fork. Do not cut it. Set aside. Slice the hard-boiled eggs about ¼ inch thick.

Cook the pasta very al dente (see page 24). Toss it in a very small amount of the tomato sauce.

¾ cup grated Romano or
Parmesan cheese
1 cup fresh or frozen tiny peas
Salt and pepper, if needed (you
may have enough from the sauce
seasoning, pasta water, etc.)

Assemble the casserole starting with a generous layer of pasta, a generous layer of shredded meat, some egg slices, some peas, some grated cheese and some sauce. Repeat, finishing with a layer of pasta. Sprinkle the top with cheese, breadcrumbs and a little more sauce. Bake in a preheated 350-degree oven for about an hour. When the top and sides are golden brown, remove from the oven and let it rest 20 minutes before serving. It may also be turned out on a plate or a cutting board and sliced as you would a cake. Extra sauce may be served, though it is neither necessary nor traditional.

NOTE: Any left over sauce will store well in the refrigerator for up to 5 days; it can also be frozen for some time. The famous Pasta N'Casciata from Ragusa in Sicily can be made simply by assembling the recipe as given. Before you place the pasta in the casserole, however, line the bottom and sides with eggplant slices cut lengthwise and fried in olive oil over high heat until golden. Let the slices cool before assembling the rest of the dish in the casserole.

Lasagne *(BAKED FILLED PASTA SHEETS)*

This could very well be the single most popular pasta dish known outside Italy. I don't personally make it often because it is so abundantly available. Whenever I do make it, I love to eat it, and I am always delighted to be served lasagne when invited out to dinner.

Wine suggested: My choice would be a good red wine like a Cabernet Sauvignon or a Chianti. However, there is nothing wrong with an equally stout white wine like a Chardonnay or an Italian Orvieto.

**1 recipe Salsa di Pomodoro Stracotto
  (Slow Tomato Sauce, see page 30)**
¾ pound ground beef
¼ pound ground pork
1 cup fresh or frozen tiny peas
**A 3-egg pasta dough (if you like,
  make spinach pasta for a change)**
Butter for greasing a baking dish
1 cup grated Parmesan cheese
1 cup shredded mozzarella cheese
Optional: 1 pound ricotta

Prepare the sauce as directed, adding the ground meat to the onion and garlic at the outset. You should cook the meat until it loses its red color before you proceed with the rest of the sauce. Add the peas to the sauce at the very end of its cooking, just before you take it off the stove.

Prepare the dough as directed on pages 13 and 14; if spinach, on page 18. Set it aside to rest.

Butter a rectangular 9-by-14-inch baking dish and set it aside.

Roll out the dough (see page 15) into large pasta sheets and dry them as directed. Then cut them into the traditional lasagne strips about 12 inches long and 1½ to 2 inches wide. A crimped pastry cutter may be used if you want a fancier edge, *or* you can cut the pieces of dough in the very old-fashioned way, using the crimped cutter and making pieces about 3 inches square, or 3 inches by 4 inches. These pieces used to be thrown into the layered casserole at random in the way you would deal a deck of cards—still a nice effect today.

Cook the pieces al dente (see page 24), a few at a time. Remove them with a slotted spoon and plunge them into cold water to stop cooking. Lay them on a damp towel.

Preheat the oven to 375 degrees.

Layer first the pasta and then the sauce alternately in the prepared casserole. If you are using ricotta, make a layer or two also, alternately with the pasta and sauce. Spread both cheeses on the top and dot with a bit more sauce. Bake for about 25 minutes. Serve piping hot.

Sformato di Pasta *(PASTA "SOUFFLÉ")*

A sformato, which simply means molded, is different from a soufflé in that it is usually turned out of its mold and onto a plate. You can do that with this dish if you like. It does not rise as much as a typical soufflé. It makes a luscious and delicate first course, even more elegant in individual ovenproof ramekins. I believe this must be a relatively new recipe because I can't imagine the old-time Italians going to such pains with a perfectly good dish of pasta. Your guests are bound to enjoy this.

Wine suggested: A light, fruity white wine like a California chablis would be a good choice. You might even try a Gewürtztraminer.

A 2-egg pasta dough, white or green
1 cup Balsamella
(White Sauce, see page 34)
1 tablespoon butter
1 small shallot, finely chopped
½ pound boiled ham, finely chopped
¾ cup grated Parmesan cheese
Salt and pepper to taste
Generous grating fresh nutmeg
5 whole eggs, separated
Butter for greasing a soufflé dish

Prepare dough as directed in the basic method (see page 14). Cut into fettucine. Set aside.

Prepare a thick Balsamella sauce as directed. Set aside.

Melt the butter in a heavy pan and add the shallot. Cook until the shallot is transparent.

Add the ham and stir. Add the grated cheese, salt and pepper and the nutmeg and stir all again. Let the mixture cool completely.

Cook the fettucine al dente (see page 24), and let it cool. Then add the ham mixture, the egg yolks and the Balsamella sauce. Mix together thoroughly.

Butter a 3- to 3½-quart soufflé dish generously. Preheat the oven to 375 degrees.

Beat the egg whites until they are stiff and shiny. Fold them carefully into the pasta mixture and pour it into the soufflé dish. Bake in the middle of the oven for about 40 minutes, or until the soufflé has risen and turned a lovely light brown. Serve immediately.

Vermicelli al Forno *(ULTRATHIN PASTA, BAKED)*

My own family have grown very fond of this dish served as a delicate first-course pasta. We do it sformato, *turned out of individual ovenproof ramekins onto a light tomato sauce covering the center of a small plate. It makes a decorative and tasty starter for an "important" meal. With the distinctive taste of the slightly bitter black olives, it is particularly good before an entree with a strong flavor, such as roasted or braised fowl or game.*

    Wine suggested: A Chardonnay or a Pinot Grigio.

Butter for greasing a casserole
8 Sicilian or Calamata black olives,
  pitted and coarsely chopped
4 slices of prosciutto, finely chopped
A few large capers, chopped
3-4 tablespoons breadcrumbs
⅓ cup chopped parsley
Olive oil, for cooking and blending
Salt and pepper to taste
12 ounces vermicelli
2 whole eggs, beaten
⅓ cup grated Parmesan cheese
Optional: 1 cup Salsa al Pomodoro
  (Quick Tomato Sauce, page 31),
  plus a spoonful or two of
  heavy cream

Prepare a small ovenproof casserole, or individual ovenproof dishes that will just hold all the ingredients, by buttering very well. Set aside.

Preheat the oven to 400 degrees. Make the "sauce" by putting the olives, prosciutto, capers, breadcrumbs, parsley and some olive oil and salt and pepper into a frying pan to cook gently. Just heat everything through to blend the flavors. Set aside.

Meanwhile, cook the pasta al dente, being very careful because this pasta is very thin and cooks very quickly. Drain it well and toss it in a little olive oil to keep it from sticking together. Then add the "sauce" and mix thoroughly. Put the mixture into the prepared casserole or individual dishes. Pour over the beaten eggs and sprinkle on the grated Parmesan.

Place the casserole or dishes in the hot oven and bake about 15 minutes or so. What you are seeking is a lovely golden crust on the top, and with luck also on the sides. Remove from the oven and allow to rest for a few minutes. You may serve it from the casserole or turned out onto the optional light tomato sauce. Or, if it is well set up, you could turn it out onto a plate and cut it up like a pie.

Pasta in Broths and Soups

(Pasta in Brodo e Minestre)

BROWN AND WHITE STOCKS

If you are not used to making homemade stock as a regular kitchen procedure, be advised that many home cooks feel you can't run a kitchen without it. Basic white stock is made simply by cooking chicken or veal bones with onion, carrot and such greens and trimmings as you may have, in plenty of water, over low heat unsalted for a long time. Brown stock is made by first roasting veal or beef bones for an hour in an oven at high heat with onion and carrot to develop color; then you place the bones and pan drippings in the stock pot together with greens and trimmings and enough water to cover, and cook over low heat unsalted for a long time. In either case, after you have strained and defatted the finished stock, it can be reduced and intensified by another period of cooking over medium-high heat without a lid.

Tagliatelle Rosa *(FRESH PASTA WITH BOILED BEEF TONGUE)*   *Serves 6*

This minestra, characteristically Italian, certainly makes a full meal when followed by salad and fruit, and it is a very nice way to enjoy a specialty meat.

1 pound fresh ribbon pasta
1 tablespoon olive oil
A little pork fat (size of a walnut)
1 medium-size onion, finely chopped
8 ounces boiled fresh beef tongue,
   cut in julienne strips
1½-2 quarts chicken or veal broth
Salt and pepper to taste
Optional: Substitute 4 ounces
   shredded prosciutto for half the
   quantity of tongue; or use only 4
   ounces prosciutto, shredded

Prepare a 3-egg dough as described on page 13.

Put the olive oil and fat into a frying pan and cook the onion in it gently until it is soft and translucent.

Add the tongue and cook for a couple of minutes more.

Next, decide whether to cook your pasta in the broth or separately in plain water. If you have an abundance of good stock, you may want the extra benefit of cooking your pasta in it, especially if it is fresh pasta and will cook quickly. Be prepared in that case for the pasta to absorb and take up some of the liquid and reduce the volume of stock.

If, on the other hand, you are short of stock or broth, and especially if you are using commercial dried pasta instead of the fresh, you are probably best advised to cook the pasta separately in plain water to the al dente stage (see page 24) and then add it to the soup.

In either case, bring the broth to a boil and add the cooked onion and tongue. Then either add and cook the raw pasta in the stock, or cook it separately and add it cooked. Pour all into a warm tureen and serve hot as a first course or as the main dish of a light meal.

Pastina in Brodo *(LITTLE PASTA CUTS IN BROTH)* *Serves 6*

This soup is sometimes called Zuppa Maritata. I guess the pasta is "married" to the broth, but in any case, this is a rich and satisfying way to start a meal. This soup approach is so simple that it demands a really good broth.

If you make your own chicken broth, there is nothing you could possibly do to improve it more than adding some chicken feet, if you can find them. They give a really rich, fresh chicken taste to the stock, and it's really too bad that they are removed from most chickens sold to American consumers. My parents always kept their own chickens, and as a child my job was to cut the entrails with scissors and clean them so that even the guts could go into the stock pot. I often wondered why, but today when I recall my mother's beautiful velvety chicken broth, I am sure she knew a great deal that the world has since forgotten.

If you cannot make your own chicken stock, you can still make a quart of tinned chicken broth much tastier by adding a celery branch cut in medium-sized pieces, a medium-size onion cut into six pieces, skin and all, three or four whole black peppercorns and a small bay leaf. Simmer the broth for about 40 minutes until you get a 20 percent reduction in volume and strain through a fine sieve or wet cheesecloth. Once you get used to these good flavors, you'll find they are worth any amount of extra trouble.

You can also use veal or beef broth in this recipe with delicious results.

1½ quarts strong chicken broth, well seasoned but clear
¾ cup pastina (see page 22)
2 tablespoons grated Parmesan cheese

Once again you must decide if you have enough extra broth to cook the pastina in, or whether you need to conserve the broth by cooking the pasta separately in plain water and adding it already cooked. In the case of this particular soup, I believe you will get a better result if you have plenty of stock and cook the pasta in it.

Bring the broth to a simmer.

Add the pastina and stir well. Let it simmer for about 6 or 7 minutes.

Serve the soup hot with about a teaspoonful of grated cheese sprinkled on top of each portion.

Tortellini in Brodo *(TORTELLINI IN BROTH)*

Serves 8

This lovely soup is traditionally served in Bologna during the Christmas holidays, and a good choice it is! Made well, it would bring joy to any eater's heart. Followed by a piece of simple roast chicken and a nice salad, this soup sets the stage for a marvelous meal indeed.

2½ quarts broth
½ recipe tortellini (see page 52)
1 cup grated Parmesan cheese

A good beef broth with some chicken added would give you broth more like that served in Bologna. Remember that Bologna is also the home of *bollito misto* (mixed boiled dinner). The Bolognese are expert at extracting essences, esters, nectars, infusions—the many ways in which good natural flavors can be captured in rich-tasting stocks. These are very often the best parts of the foods from which they are made. You will need a generous amount of whichever stock you choose for this dish, because the fresh tortellini should be cooked in it and they will absorb a fair amount.

Bring the broth to a simmer.

Add the tortellini and cook just until they are tender.

Serve the soup hot and pass the grated cheese at the table.

Minestrone alla Genovese (SOUP GENOA STYLE) Serves 10 or more

It is very sad that the "minestrone" served in a lot of restaurants in America is heavy, mushy, water-logged and tastes as though it has been reheated for days on end. Until you have sampled a freshly made Minestrone alla Genovese with each vegetable crisply and separately defined, you won't know what a minestrone actually is and can be. Even a person with limited cooking experience can tell from reading the recipe that this soup should be made fresh and consumed at once in order to be eaten at its best.

The fresh basil in this recipe indicates that it is generally made in the late summer or early fall when the herb is in season. However, it can still be made in winter by using fresh or frozen stored pesto or dried basil. Note that it is practically a vegetarian dish, which is characteristic of the way you would find it in Italy, where an abundance of fresh in-season vegetables is as common as meat is scarce.

Minestrone at its best is a rib-sticking soup that could easily be the mainstay of a delicious meal if you add some crusty bread, a simple green salad and some fresh fruit and cheese.

Wine suggested: A white wine such as a Sauvignon Blanc would be very good with this dish.

1 cup finely chopped carrots
1 cup finely chopped onions
2 cups peeled and finely chopped
   raw potatoes
2 cups finely chopped spinach or
   swiss chard
3 quarts water
2 cups dry white beans, presoaked
   overnight in cold water
Salt to taste
½ teaspoon finely ground
   black pepper
½ pound small macaroni
¼ cup finely chopped parsley
3 leaves fresh basil, finely chopped
3 ounces prosciutto fat, or
   3 ounces pancetta, or
   3 ounces bacon, blanched to
   remove the smoky flavor;
   finely chopped
2 cloves garlic, well crushed
½ cup grated Parmesan cheese

Put the first eight ingredients into a pot and bring to a simmer. Cook gently until all is well blended and the beans are al dente.

Now in the case of minestrone or other such soups which you want to be thick, you probably should cook the pasta in them, as it would take up some of the volume of liquid. If the soup then becomes too thick, you can add some boiling water or broth, but it should not be too thin, either. At this point, therefore, add the pasta and cook until it is barely al dente.

When ready to serve the minestrone, mash together the parsley, basil, fat and garlic in a food processor, blender or mortar and pestle. When it has become a nice thick mass, add it to the minestrone and stir well.

Serve the minestrone piping hot and pass some grated cheese at the table.

Pasta e Fagioli *(PASTA AND BEANS)*

This dish is famous as "pasta fazool," and it can be made in many ways. Some regional variations of the basic recipe are given in the Note. Again, this is practically a vegetarian dish and a hearty one, particularly suited to cold weather. Followed by some fresh fruit and cheese, it makes a good meal that is also good for you.

2 cups dried white cannellini or Great Northern beans
1 ounce prosciutto including skin, or 1 ounce lean salt pork
1 large onion, medium diced
2 garlic cloves, peeled and well mashed
¼ cup olive oil
Salt to taste
¼ teaspoon freshly ground black pepper
Cold water to cover the beans
½ pound small short macaroni
¼ cup grated Parmesan cheese

Place all the ingredients except the pasta and grated cheese in a small stock pot. Bring to a simmer and cook gently until the beans are soft but not mushy.

If the water is all absorbed, add more boiling water or some stock. Remember that the pasta will absorb some of the liquid, unless you cook it separately in plain water.

Add the pasta and cook until it is just done, not mushy. The soup should be quite dense.

Serve it hot and pass grated cheese as well as the pepper mill for individual grindings of fresh black pepper.

NOTE: For a Tuscan version of this soup, add a good cup of coarsely chopped fresh or canned tomatoes. For a Venetian version use red kidney beans instead of the white, and a nice pinch of cinnamon.

Pallotoline in Brodo *(TINY MEATBALLS AND PASTINA IN BROTH)* Serves 6

It should be evident by now that the quality of the thin Italian soups or broths depends greatly upon using a superlative basic stock from either fowl or meat, while the thick minestrones are more apt to be made simply with good fresh vegetables. It seems fitting to end this section with one of the most elegant and popular soups of all. In order to make it there is really no adequate substitute for best homemade velvety veal stock.

Plain toasted Italian bread is good with this soup. It makes a lovely plain lunch or supper or a good midnight snack, or a small portion can be served as the first course of a large meal. My family calls it "invalid" soup, as it's a perfect thing to make and send around to sick friends who can't cook for themselves.

1½ quarts best-quality homemade veal stock
8-9 ounces ground veal
3 tablespoons grated Parmesan cheese
3 tablespoons fine dry breadcrumbs
1 teaspoon finely minced shallot
Salt and pepper to taste
1 large whole egg
4-5 ounces dried pastina (see page 22)
Optional: A few teaspoons finely minced parsley, added to meatball ingredients or sprinkled on top of the soup

Put the broth in a large saucepan over low heat and let it slowly come up to a simmer.

Meanwhile, combine the veal, cheese, breadcrumbs, shallot, salt and pepper and egg in a bowl and mix thoroughly. Roll the mixture into tiny balls about the size of hazelnuts. This may seem like thankless work, but the results will justify it. The meatballs can also be made in advance. You can even make up a large amount and freeze some of them, spreading them out on a sheet to freeze separately before putting them in a freezer wrap. This will enable you to make this soup at a moment's notice.

When the meatballs are shaped and ready and the broth is simmering, taste the broth to make sure it is delicious and correct it for seasoning as needed. Start to drop in the meatballs, a few at a time. As they cook through, they will rise to the top of the broth and stay there. Allow the last ones you drop to cook for 3 or 4 minutes, then reduce the heat to keep the soup just warm.

Meanwhile, cook the pastina separately al dente (see page 24). Warm the soup bowls and put a generous spoonful of pastina in the bottom of each bowl.

Serve up the soup and pass extra grated cheese at the table; but do not let anyone smother this soup's delicate flavors by adding too much cheese.

Fried Pasta

(Pasta Fritti)

Panzarotti *(FRIED RAVIOLI)*   *Serves 6*

These tasty little morsels can be filled with other things you might have on hand such as chopped meat or vegetables. They are delicious just as a snack, or as an appetizer with drinks before dinner. They can also make an unusual first course. Use your imagination both in serving and filling them. My own favorite is a filling of ricotta, which is delicious in any form.

Wine suggested: Zinfandel is a good choice to accompany this dish, as is Chianti, too.

A 3-egg pasta dough (see page 13)
1 pound ricotta
3 ounces prosciutto, finely chopped
¼ cup finely chopped parsley
Salt and pepper to taste
1 whole egg
Olive oil for frying

Prepare the dough as directed. Set it aside to rest.

Mix together the cheese, prosciutto, parsley, salt and pepper and egg. Set the mixture aside.

Roll out the pasta into thin, large sheets. Do not let them dry out. You can cut and fill these in squares as for ravioli (see page 54), or in rounds as for agnolotti (see page 55). For this recipe I prefer the rounds, also called ravioli in some parts of Italy.

Cut the pasta sheet into rounds 2½ inches in diameter, using a cookie cutter or a glass. Put a good teaspoon of the filling on top of each one. Fold the dough over to look like a turnover and pinch the edges together to make a tight seal, using a wash of beaten egg to make it stick, if necessary.

Fry the panzarotti in very hot oil until golden and crisp. Serve immediately.

Frittata di Spaghetti *(SPAGHETTI OMELETTE)*

This is another good way to use leftover pasta. It is a great brunch dish and makes a very nice first course. It is probably at its very best as a midnight snack. You can add other ingredients, too, such as anchovies, capers, or tuna fish to suit your taste.

Wine suggested: A Cabernet Sauvignon or a Montepulciano d'Abruzzo would be my choice with this dish.

3 tablespoons olive oil
12 ounces cold cooked pasta, such as spaghetti, vermicelli or linguine
3 eggs
½ cup grated Parmesan cheese
Salt and pepper to taste
¼ cup finely chopped parsley
¼ cup finely chopped Gaeta or Calamata black olives

Put the oil in a wide, heavy frying pan over medium heat.

When it is very hot (though long before it starts to smoke) add the pasta. Spread it in the pan in a nice round, flat shape about 1½ inches high.

Leave it to cook slowly for about 5 or 6 minutes until it is golden on the bottom. Watch that it does not burn.

Beat the eggs and add to them the cheese, salt and pepper, parsley and black olives. Pour this mixture over the pasta in the pan and gently poke it into the mass of pasta with a fork. Lower the heat.

As soon as the eggs have set, turn a dish over on top of the omelette. Invert the pan to remove the omelette to the plate. Then gently slide the omelette off the plate and back into the frying pan and let it brown on the other side.

You can eliminate this last maneuver by placing the frying pan with the pasta under a preheated broiler until the top browns. It must be watched carefully, however, so that it does not burn or dry out.

When the pasta omelette is done, turn it out of the pan onto a board or serving platter. Let it rest for about 5 minutes. Cut it in wedges and serve hot, or tepid, as is done in Italy.

Crocchetti di Spaghetti *(PASTA CROQUETTES)*

This is a very attractive and delicious way to use up leftover pasta. These croquettes can be excellent with roast beef, chicken or broiled lamb chops.
  Wine suggested: A Petite Sirah or a Valpolicella.

1 pound leftover cooked pasta, such as spaghetti, tagliatelle or just about anything
4-5 ounces leftover meat or chicken, shredded
1 cup thick Balsamella (White Sauce, see page 34)
⅓ cup grated Parmesan cheese
⅓ cup tomato sauce (either quick, page 31, or slow-cooked, page 30)
Salt and pepper to taste
Flour, as needed, for rolling out
Beaten egg, as needed, for rolling out
Fine breadcrumbs, as needed, for rolling out
Olive oil for frying

Grease a shallow baking pan, having sides at least an inch high, with olive oil. Set it aside.

Mix together in a saucepan the pasta, meat, white sauce, Parmesan cheese, tomato sauce and salt and pepper to taste. Heat the mixture through and stir until it is well amalgamated.

Pour the mixture into the baking pan and spread it out evenly with a spatula. It should be about 1¼ inches high. Let it cool thoroughly, in the refrigerator if necessary, so that it will set solidly.

Cut it out in shapes you like with a knife or cookie cutter. Regular bars will do very well. Roll the cutouts in flour, then in beaten egg, and then in breadcrumbs, pressing them down all over to make sure they thoroughly cover the surface.

Heat ½ inch of olive oil in a frying pan to almost smoking hot. Carefully put in the croquettes and cook until golden brown. Watch them to make sure they don't burn, and turn them at least once to brown on as many sides as possible.

Place the browned croquettes on draining paper set in a pan in a warm oven. You can keep them hot in a slow oven if you are planning to serve them right away. Or you can hold them back for a little while and reheat them in a preheated 325-degree oven for about 10 minutes before serving. Leave the door of the oven slightly ajar so that they won't steam and become soggy.

This dish makes an unusual and distinctive first course. It could be followed by roast veal with pan juices, green beans or broccoli, some cheese and a bowl of fruit. It can also be a very friendly and warming dish to eat late at night. After a movie or an opera, when you get a case of the munchies but want something more substantial and with a bit of style, this dish can do a good job of filling the bill. I have even eaten pasta fritta for breakfast when I couldn't face cereal or bacon and eggs.

Wine suggested: My choice with this dish, served at any hour (except, perhaps, breakfast), is a nice Zinfandel, or a bottle of red Corvo.

12 ounces cooked pasta, a long ribbon cut, or even the fine capelli d'angelo
⅓ cup olive oil, or a little more
8-9 anchovy fillets, finely chopped
⅓ cup grated Romano cheese
Freshly ground black pepper
A pinch red pepper flakes
4 tablespoons chopped parsley

You can make this fresh according to the basic directions in the front of the book, but it is also a good occasion for using up any leftover pasta you may have.

Heat half of the oil in a frying pan and add the anchovies. Cook for about 3 minutes, stirring all the time. Add the anchovies and oil to the cooked pasta in a bowl and mix well.

Add the cheese, black pepper, and red pepper flakes to the pasta mixture and toss thoroughly.

Put the rest of the olive oil in the frying pan. When it is fairly hot, add the pasta mixture and spread it into a round shape about 1½ inches high. Fry it gently until the bottom is set and golden brown.

Put a plate on top of the pasta, face down. Carefully invert the pan, leaving the pasta on the plate. Then slide the pasta back into the pan with the uncooked side down and gently fry it until it is golden.

Remove the fried pasta from the pan onto a warm plate. Sprinkle on the chopped parsley, cut the pasta into wedges and serve it hot.

Sweets

(Dolce)

Tortelli di Ricotta *(RICOTTA "PILLOWS")*   *Serves 8*

This dish is simple but very festive. You can make the tortelli well in advance and put them in a single layer on a floured cloth, lightly covered with plastic wrap, in the refrigerator. When you are ready to serve them, proceed as directed and enjoy.

   Wine suggested: A Johannisberg Riesling or a Moscato d'Asti.

A 3-egg pasta dough (see page 13)
2 tablespoons olive oil
A pinch of salt

FILLING:
½ pound ricotta cheese
2 eggs
4 ounces granulated sugar
5 tablespoons dark rum
Beaten egg, as needed
Olive oil for frying
Superfine sugar

Prepare the dough as directed, but add 2 tablespoons of olive oil and a pinch of salt. Set aside.

   Mix the ricotta, eggs, sugar and rum. Set aside.

   Roll out the pasta dough as thin as possible in large sheets. Cut out circles about 3 inches in diameter. Put a good teaspoonful of the filling on each. Fold the circles over like turnovers and press the edges together, using beaten egg or water to make them stick. At this point they can be held back and stored in the refrigerator if desired.

   When ready to serve, heat the oil to about 375 degrees. Add the tortelli and fry until golden. Drain on absorbent paper and sprinkle with superfine sugar.

   Place the tortelli in a flameproof dish. Heat a little rum, being careful not to let it boil. Pour the hot rum around the edges of the tortelli, ignite with a match and serve. Be careful not to burn the tortelli, the sprinkled sugar—or the guests!

Cuscinetti di Teramo

(FRIED "CUSHIONS" WITH SWEETMEAT STUFFING)   *Makes about 20*

This recipe and the ones that follow in this section are examples of the further evolution of the ancient Roman and Italian pasta into the category of sweet-tooth delicacies. I am including them in this collection because the methods, tools and even shapes used are so similar to those used in the basic pasta that those who have mastered the one should feel quite sanguine about trying their hands at the other. We must return full circle to the first definition of the word "pasta," meaning simply a paste of flour and liquid. Depending on how we handle this paste, it can also become the basis for making simple pastries.

Wine suggested: A Moscato or an Asti Spumante.

1 cup all-purpose flour
Pinch of salt
3 tablespoons granulated sugar
4 tablespoons olive oil
2-3 tablespoons Marsala or
   dry red wine
4 tablespoons grape or apricot jam
2 ounces bitter chocolate, grated
⅓ cup chopped toasted almonds
Peanut oil for frying
Honey

Place the flour on a pastry board. Make a "well" and add the salt, sugar, olive oil and enough wine to make a firm but tender dough. Knead it well; it is not necessary to knead it a long time. Roll out in a large thin sheet and cut into rounds about 3 inches in diameter.

Mix the chocolate, nuts and jam together. Place a little of this mixture on each circle of dough. Fold each circle over like a turnover. Moisten the edges with milk or a little beaten egg and press them shut with your fingers or a fork.

Heat the peanut oil to about 350 degrees in a frying pan and fry the "cushions" until they are deep golden in color. Drain them on paper towels, brush with honey and serve hot or cold.

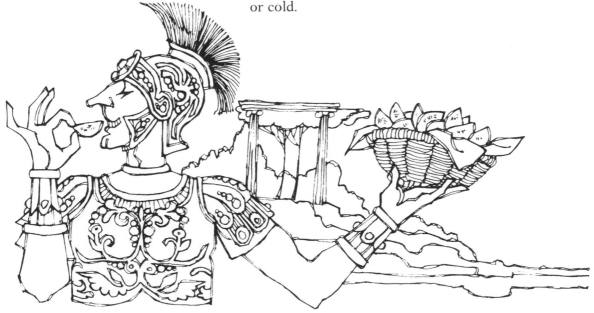

Cannoli Siciliana *(FILLED TUBES OF PASTRY)*

Makes about 24

These are the world-famous and popular Cannoli, said to have originated in Sicily from the time of the Arab invasion. I doubt that many people who enjoy these toothsome treats realize they are yet another form of pasta, ingeniously deep fried and shaped to become an elegant confection.

CANNOLI:
2 cups all-purpose flour
½ teaspoon salt
2 tablespoons lard or shortening
1 tablespoon granulated sugar
½-¾ cup dry Marsala
1 egg, slightly beaten
1 quart frying oil (peanut
    is good, olive oil is traditional)

FILLING:
2 pounds ricotta cheese
¾ cup confectioners' sugar
2-3 tablespoons finely chopped
    assorted glacéed fruit
4 tablespoons finely chopped
    semi-sweet chocolate
A few drops heavy cream, as
    needed to soften the cheese
Optional: Chopped pistachio nuts
    or maraschino cherries for
    decorating; vanilla, rum or
    Cointreau flavoring

My father used to make cannoli on the end of an old broom handle. It's easier if you find tubes of bamboo or the metal ones specially made for cannoli, which are 5 inches long by about 1 inch in diameter.

Place the flour on a board or pastry marble. Make a "well" and add the salt, shortening and sugar. Add a little wine and start mixing as you would for pie dough. The amount of wine you use will depend upon the flour absorption. Use as much as the dough will take. Keep mixing until you have a soft ball that is not crumbly. Then knead the dough for about 7 or 8 minutes until it is slightly glossy.

Cover it and set it aside for about an hour. Do not refrigerate unless you intend to hold it over for use the next day. In this case be sure to take it out in plenty of time for it to reach room temperature, or it will be too firm to work.

Cut the dough into 2 pieces. Roll these out as thin as possible with a rolling pin or a pasta machine. Cut 4-inch rounds with a cookie cutter, or cut 4-inch squares by hand with a knife. (I prefer the rounds because they will display the filling so attractively.)

Wrap each piece of cut dough around a cannoli tube. Overlap the two edges and seal with a little bit of slightly beaten egg. Make as many as you have tubes to work with.

Preheat the frying oil to 375 degrees. Drop in the prepared tubes 2 at a time. They cook very quickly in about 1 minute, so don't neglect them. Fry the tubes until golden brown, then remove them from the oil with long tongs, a slotted spoon or even a pair of clean pliers. Set them on a dish with paper towels to drain off the extra oil.

Wait about 10 seconds and then pick up the tube with a pair of pliers. (They will be extremely hot, so watch out!) With a thick kitchen towel carefully grasp the cannoli and pull the tube out. Stack the cannoli shells on a dish with towels beneath them. When the tubes are cool enough to handle, repeat the process until you have used up all of the circles or squares of dough.

Cannoli shells freeze beautifully, so you can make a lot of them when you have the time and then freeze them carefully wrapped. You can also store them outside the refrigerator in an airtight container for at least 10 to 14 days. If they become slightly stale (they won't unless you use stale oil, so make *sure* it is not rancid), place them in a preheated 325-degree oven for about 4 minutes. Cool and use. Do *not* fill them ahead of time or they will become soggy.

Mix together the ricotta, sugar, fruit and chocolate, using just enough cream to make it soft but not runny. *Just before serving*, pipe the filling into the cannoli shells. A pastry bag is the easiest and fastest to use; a spoon or knife is much slower. Decorate the ends with bits of pistachio, cherry, or chocolate. Place them in cupcake papers so they won't roll about, and sprinkle liberally with confectioners' sugar. They should be eaten out of hand.

Made properly, these will be light as a feather, flaky and melt-in-the-mouth. The filling is not too sweet. I've had guests devour dozens each at one sitting!

Cenci *("RAGS")*

The traditional recipe for Cenci, or "rags," includes eggs added to a basic dough similar to the cannoli dough. The odd or irregular shape accounts for the name. However, I make cenci from the cannoli dough trimmings, or the scraps I have left after cutting out the rounds for my cannoli. I find that most people prefer them in this plain dough without the eggs.

Simply deep fry the leftover dough scraps in the peanut oil after you have finished the cannoli; lift them out and drain on paper towels; then sprinkle them with confectioners' sugar. They make a lovely dessert with fruit, berries or ice cream. The bowl of cenci thus made disappears from my kitchen in no time flat every time I make cannoli.

Wine suggested: With either the cannoli or the cenci and fruit, I would select a late harvest Johannisberg Riesling or an Orvieto Abbocato.

Wines (VINI)

Any remarks I make about wines, whether they be Italian, French or Californian, should be taken with a fifth of the stuff, as it will make it all easier and better. Of wines I know not a great deal. Mostly the knowledge extends to remembering what I have liked in the past as to type and to trying to get more as I want it. I also "know" by some genetic programming what is acceptable in Italian wines, and this enables me to enjoy almost all of them for their own characteristics and on their own merits.

Not being a wine scholar and, I might add, not having a good memory, I find it especially difficult to discuss wines except in the most general terms, probably best expressed as a wine-drinking philosophy. Those of my colleagues who have vast experience and knowledge of wine-making and wine-drinking are blessed, according to them, with good memories. Therefore, when they speak of wines, they can often say, quite accurately, "This wine is not as good as the '68, which was also grown on the southeast slope of the highest hill in the vineyard." Of course all these factors do make a difference in the wine at drinking time.

Then there is the method of making the stuff. Steel tanks, controlled fermentation, killing off wild yeast and introducing a new one which, like DNA, will give you certain predictable characteristics. Can you imagine what progress is doing to the wine industry? You'll soon be able to order up a 1985 Vintage with blue eyes and blond hair. This is the science of wine-making and drinking. I will talk mostly about the soul of wine-drinking.

The Italians are fast adapting the wine-growing and wine-making that the French and Californians have used for such a long time. They want to compete on more objective grounds with the French and California wines. Italy currently supplies so much wine to the French and the Americans that it seems impossible that the country could produce so much. The wine scientists are generally critical of Italian wines because they compare them to the French and California wines. This is already an error. You can't taste an orange and then complain that it just doesn't measure up to that apple eaten the other day. Italian wines are as complex as any others, but different. As long as you remember that they are different from other wines, you will be able to enjoy them on their own merits.

In Italy, wine *is* food. It is as simple as that. Italian wines tend to be a little lower in alcohol content than the wines of other countries. They are often sharper (I'd say "gutsy") and they like to be lured out into the open. As a general rule, let red wines "breathe" for at least one hour before serving. There is an Italian saying that if you want to treat your guests well, open the wine the night before you expect them.

Wine-drinking is a national pastime for sure in Italy, but there is a very low incidence of alcoholism—one of the lowest in the world. There is also very long life expectancy in Italy. I'm convinced that this is because of the pasta and wine consumption. Wine in Italy is appreciated very much on its own, but it is almost always served together with something to eat. An afternoon glassful will often be accompanied by hard, tasty cookies and a basket of fruit. When making a shopping list or making up a menu, wine is there along with the peppers, pasta, veal, cheese and bread, all equal partners in the care and happiness of the stomach and soul. You don't need to be a mathematician to calculate that in the formula of, say, $20 for a nice, homecooked meal for four people and $10 or $12 or even more for a bottle of good wine in America there is a horrible imbalance. Wine-drinking here is more of a hobby or a sport than in Italy, and, as a result, we have fewer wines available that are so priced as to be in line with other food costs. Italians would not tolerate this. Many still make their own wine at home. While I don't like wine snobs, I find nothing wrong with an Italian who generously offers a glass of his home specialty and proudly says, "I make the best!"

White wines are also enjoyed in Italy, but they are outnumbered by the reds two to one. There are more and more whites now being produced of excellent quality and low price. A bottle of chilled white wine with some prosciutto and melon or figs is sheer heaven! Fish and chicken, both eaten extensively in Italy, are easy partners to white wine. But look out! Good, deep, chest-thumping red ones are equally at home with these self-same fish and chickens. Some time when you are eating fish or chicken in a restaurant, look the waiter in the eye and say, with authority, "I want red wine," and then enjoy your meal.

For those of you who are wise scholars of good wine and good taste and good memory, think of me often and toast me with a great wine which I will probably never have (unless you give it to me). I will toast you, too, because of the time and attention you give to a very important food. We can co-exist very well. As an example of the importance of wine in the life of the Italians, I can cite the following. Italy is the largest wine producer in the world. It is also the largest wine consumer in the world. Italy produces more types and varieties of wine than any other nation, 1500 in fact. The best known of these number above 420. Italy, a tiny country with a fraction of the population of the States, produces about four times as much wine as America, and supplies more wine to America than any other foreign country. One last fact tells the story better than I can. Italy produces 2 billion gallons of wine per year (that's 10 billion fifths!). Eighteen percent of this production is exported. Eighty-two percent, or 1 billion 640 million gallons, is drunk by the Italians themselves at the rate of around 30 gallons per capita annually and by the tourists who flock to enjoy Italy's many charms.

The following is a very short list of Italian wines which I believe you will enjoy. They are merely drops in the vast ocean of Italian wines, but they are excellent wines, all worthy of your appraisal. You may want to get more acquainted with Italian wines by writing for an excellent Italian Wine Guide brochure put out by the Italian Wine Promotion Center, 499 Park Avenue, New York, N.Y. 10022 (212-980-1100), available free of charge.

Barolo–A big dry red wine, made from the Nebbiolo grape, that needs age. It is best after 10 years. A great wine in every way. One of the best of the Piedmont region.

Barbera–Made from the same Nebbiolo grape, but made near the town of Barbera. Less alcoholic than Barolo, but very good, strong character. Dry and full-bodied with red garnet color.

Asti Spumante–A sparkling champagne-like wine made from the Moscato grape in Asti, Piedmont. It is semi-sweet with an amber color, and perfect for desserts of fresh fruit, especially peaches, with dry cakes or cookies.

Valpolicella–A wine from the Veneto region around Verona. Made mainly from Corvina, Rondinella and Molinara grapes, it is red, warm, smooth and dry with a touch of sweetness.

Soave–The famous white wine from Verona, known since the 13th century. Made from Garganega and Trebbiano di Soave grapes, it is dry and crisp and can be used very well with a big variety of foods.

Pinot Grigio–Grey Pinot grapes make this dry, tart, delicious white wine from the Friuli-Venezia Giulia region. Drink it before dinner as well as matching it up with pork roast and some good stout cheeses.

Chianti–Surely the most famous Tuscan wine in America. It is a marvelous wine which can be used with almost any food, or drunk just on its own. There is young Chianti made to be drunk like a Beaujolais, and of course the Riserva which is at least three years old and made from Sangiovese, Canaiolo Black and a few Malvasia grapes. It is better to let the Riserva age for four or more years before quaffing this ruby-red gem.

Vino Nobile di Montepulciano–This red wine, which was known in the 14th century, is made like the Chianti Riserva, but it must be aged at least four years. Delicious with roasts, good stout cheeses, and pears and apples.

Brunello di Montalcino–Made from Brunello grapes (a relative of Sangiovese grapes), this is a rather recent wine on the Italian scene, being only around 100 years old. It is quite expensive and must be barrel-aged at least four years before being bottled. It could easily age 50 years thereafter, but don't wait. Use it as you would a Chianti Riserva.

Verdicchio–From the Marches region we have a lovely crisp white wine made mostly from Verdicchio grapes. It has been noted for its quality since Roman times. Its bottle has the characteristic fish shape which you may have seen. When you are that old you can afford to be whimsical! It is delicious with fish or roasted game birds. I like it with polenta.

Orvieto–Umbria gives us two types of this white wine, the one dry, intense and clear, and the other, the Abbocato, very fruity with a lovely aftertaste. They are both made from the Trebbiano grape with some Tuscan Malvasia, Verdello and Grechetto. There is red, but you are not likely to encounter it.

The dry white is good with a variety of dishes. The Abbocato would be good with Gorgonzola cheese.

Frascati–The Castelli Romani (Roman Castles) area around Rome, which produces many light delicious white and red wines, gives us Frascati made from Malvasia, Tuscan Trebbiano, and Greco (yellow Trebbiano). Traditionally it was drunk very young, straight out of the barrel (some is still delivered that way in Rome from a horse-drawn wagon). What we get here is a modern version made to stand the rigors of travel across the sea. The old type is from the Renaissance times. The modern Frascati is delicate, so don't use it with highly flavored dishes.

Winemaking in Sicily is in the midst of a revolution, not a political one for a change. Sicily, being the poorest region of Italy economically, is also the last to be able to modernize its winemaking so that more reliable wines will emerge year after year. The government is now taking a hand in this, in order to help the Sicilian people, and because of the fine growing conditions on the sunny island. While few of these newly improved wines are yet finding their way to the American market, there are some that should not be overlooked. The red and white Corvo wines are excellent in taste, color and price. I use them often. If you bottle-age the red, you can get a really nice wine. It will be smooth and do a lot for the foods you serve with it. The world-famous Marsala from its namesake city is indispensable for cooking and baking. It also makes a nice *digestivo* at the end of a meal. As more wines come from Sicily with the government standard letters "D.O.C." attesting their quality on the label, the adventurous will want to try them. They will reflect the rich variety of the Sicilian cultural history. You can take my word that these wines will taste good and be good for you.

Cheeses *(FORMAGGI)*

The cheeses of Italy are as varied and complex as the wines and far more difficult to discuss. One can start by saying that the Italians have not traditionally been large milk drinkers, which may stem from earlier lack of facilities for pasteurization. However, they make up for it by eating a great deal of many different types of cheese. Furthermore, they milk not only cows, but also sheep, goats and even water buffaloes in order to produce a wide variety of cheeses.

Availability of these cheeses in America is also a problem linked to regulations around pasteurization and aging required for import. It is slowly being worked out, and more good Italian cheeses are gradually showing up in this country. The Italians also have a lot to learn about shipping *con moto*, packing to protect their products from damage in transit, and other logistics to permit their cheeses to become a viable export product. They are more used to taking each day as it comes, and they have only recently begun to think in terms of sending their most precious, delicate and perishable products so far from home. I now believe that they are modifying some of their cheeses to enable them to travel better and longer, while still maintaining their outstanding goodness. However, the taste of Italian cheese on its home soil is still a richer and more exciting experience than sampling the export product. When you travel in Italy, I hope you will go directly to the store and buy and taste the cheese so that you will experience it at its finest.

In order to give you even a brief general discussion of Italian cheeses, it would take a big book on its own. Not this one. The following list of cheeses will give you a nice selection of those which travel best to America and a brief description of their characteristics. You are more likely to find these available than some other delicious but more obscure Italian cheeses.

Bel Paese—Cow's milk. Made also in the United States under license. The domestic one has a picture of the world on it. The imported cheese has a map of Italy. Soft, smooth, and very pleasant.

Caciotta—Sheep's milk or sometimes goat. Can be hard cheese for eating or grating. There is a soft one from Lodi which is excellent with fruit. It's a little sharp and very fragrant.

Gorgonzola—Cow's milk. The king of Italian cheeses. This famous "blue" cheese is actually green and happens naturally. It is utterly delicious with apples, pears or peaches. Wonderful to cook with, too. Sharp and fragrant and creamy-crumbly.

Mascarpone or Mascherpone—Cow's milk. This 88 percent butterfat cheese is like cheese-flavored butter. It is slightly tart, and an absolute treat, if you can get it, being especially perishable in its transit from Italy.

Mozzarella—Water buffalo milk. The imported one is very pungent, very expensive and very difficult to find. It is rather stringy and pully, used a lot in cooking and indispensable in Italian dishes.

Parmigiano–Cow's milk. Can there be two kings of cheese? If so, this is another. Utterly necessary to a majority of Italian dishes. Grated fresh or eaten in a chunk, it is pure heaven. Smooth, luscious and superbly flavored.

Pecorino–Sheep's milk. Another indispensable cheese for pastas and meat stuffings. Also known as Romano, Sardo, etc. It has a salty and forceful flavor. A great cheese.

Provolone–Water buffalo milk, and sometimes cow's. Has great fragrance and crumbly texture. A good ally in the kitchen because it brings out the flavor of other ingredients.

Ricotta–Sheep's milk, sometimes goat. In the United States it is made of cow's milk. This is another indispensable cheese in Italian cooking. It is equally at home in a pasta dish like lasagne or ravioli, or in a dessert like cannoli or ricotta pudding. Lovely-tasting and so versatile.

Robiola–Goat's milk. This northern Italian cheese is fresh, soft and creamy. Sometimes it is runny. It is piquant, yet smooth, and has a wonderful after-taste. Good with pears and apples and bread.

Taleggio (Stracchino)–Cow's milk. Specific cheese from its namesake city near Bergamo. One of many *stracca* or "tired" cheeses. Supposedly the cows moved from pasture to pasture and became tired. When milked, they gave good but different-tasting milk. It was probably the different grasses they ate rather than their state of fatigue that made the change. This cheese is soft, creamy and almost nutty in flavor. It is an excellent eating cheese and a good companion to almost anything you want.